Organic Chemistry Advanced Basics

By

Dr Mahanklhali Venu Chary Black Smith

Dedicated to Lord Shri Lakshmi Narasimha Swamy

Organic Chemistry Advanced Basics

Back to School

Published by:
Dr M Venu Chary Ph D
Venus Academy

ISBN-10: 1096771888
ISBN-13: 978-1096771883
ASIN: B07RG99XRY
Sold by: Amazon Digital Services LLC
Available: Amazon online Book store

Acknowledgements

I take this opportunity to express a deep sense of gratitude towards my son M Vrajesh Chary for his invaluable contribution to the creation of this book. I am also thankful to my daughter, 'Shree Shpoorti' who has always motivated me by her innocent and playful nature.

I convey sincere thanks to my parents Mr. M Vittala Chary and Mrs. M Kannamma (late). I am extremely thankful to Mrs. Renuka M Sc, B Ed. who was kind enough to give valuable suggestions regarding contents of this book.

Finally, I am thankful to you for reading this book. I am sure this book will make a creative and constructive contribution to your preparation for all Chemistry Exams.

Dr M Venu Chary
M Sc, Ph D (IICT)

Contents	Page
1. Structure of Organic Molecules	05

    1.1. Hybridization (SP3, SP2, SP)
    1.2. Bond Length
    1.3. Bond Angle
    1.4. Bond Energy

2. Reactivity of Organic Molecules   22

    2.1. Bond fission (Homolytic, Heterolytic)
    2.2. Types of Reagents
        Free radicals, Electrophiles, Nucleophiles
    2.3. Types of Reactions and Mechanism
    2.4. Substitution Reactions
        Free Radical, Electrophilic, Nucleophilic (SN1, SN2, SNi)
    2.5. Addition Reactions
        Free Radical, Electrophilic, Nucleophilic
    2.6. Elimination Reactions (E1, E2)
    2.7. Molecular Rearrangements
    2.8. Pericyclic Reactions

3. Electronic Displacement   44

    3.1. Inductive Effect (permanent effect)
    3.2. Mesomeric Effect (permanent effect)
    3.3. Inductomeric Effect (temporary effect)
    3.4. Electromeric Effect (temporary effect)
    3.5. Hyperconjugation

4. Acidity and Basicity   59

    4.1. Acidity of Carboxylic Acids
    4.2. Acidity of Phenols
    4.3. Acidity of Alcohols
    4.4. Acidity of Alkynes
    4.5. Basicity concept
    4.6. Basicity of Aliphatic Amines
    4.7. Basicity of Aromatic Amines
    4.8. Basicity of Amides, Imines and Cyanides

5. Isomerism and Stereochemistry Basics   73

    5.1 Classification of Isomers
        Normal Isomers
        Structural Isomers (Chain, Positional, Functional, Metamers, Ring Chain)
        Stereo Isomers (Enantiomers, Diastereomers)
    5.2. Dynamic Isomers: Structural and Stereoisomers

6. Stereochemistry Advanced   83

    6.1. Chirality and Optical Activity
    6.2. Enantiomers and Diastereomers
    6.3. Configuration (Relative and Absolute)
    6.4. CIP Rules (E/Z and R/S Nomenclature)

    6.5. Chapter wise sample problems and solutions   **105**

1. Structure of Organic Molecules

Valency of carbon: number of unpaired electrons in valence shell
Ground state electronic configuration: $1s^2\ 2s^2\ 2p_x^1\ 2p_y^1\ 2p_z^0$
   Calculated valency: 2
   Observed valency: 4

Excited state electronic configuration: $1s^2\ 2s^1\ 2p_x^1\ 2p_y^1\ 2p_z^1$
without octet configuration which is unstable /less stable
   :CH_2 - carbene valency = 2
   :CCl_2 – dichloro carbene valency = 2
   With octet configuration which is more stable
   CH_4 – methane valency = 4
   CCl_4 – carbon tetrachloride valency = 4

After exciting carbon will have half filled stable configuration.
   Examples of valency 2: :CH_2 carbene, :CHCl monochlorocarbene, :CCl_2 dichlorocarbene, :CHBr mono bromocarbene, :CBr_2 dibromocarbene, :CF_2 difluorocarbene.
Formation of CH_4

$2s^1$ $2p_x^1$ $2p_y^1$ $2p_z^1$

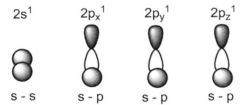

s - s   s - p   s - p   s - p

But this type of formation is not taking place

1.1. Hybridization

Hybridization: Hybridization takes place within the atom by overlapping the orbitals. The phenomenon of mixing up of dissimilar orbital of an atom having nearly same energy and redistribution of their energy to farm same number of new orbitals of identical shape and equivalent energies is known as hybridization.

SP³ – Hybridization:

Tetrahedral shape, e.g. Methane (CH_4), saturated hydrocarbons e.g. Alkanes, alcohols, cycloalkanes and their derivatives.

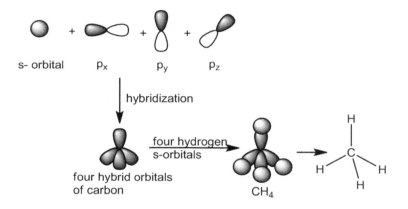

For example:

H H
H–C=C–H
H H
Ethane
all are σ bonds

H H
C=C
H H
Ethylene
five σ bonds
one π bond

σ = sigma bond
π = pi bond

Hybridization takes place for the sake of stability.
Types of hybridization: (1) sp³ (2) sp² (3) sp

SP² – Hybridization:
Trigonal planar

s- orbital   p- orbitals   sp² hybridization

Ethylene (C_2H_4)

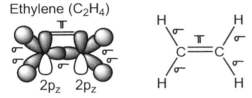

five 'σ' bonds and one 'π' bond
σ = sigma bond; π = pi bond

Unsaturated alkenes, benzene and their derivatives

SP – Hybridization:
Linear in shape e.g. Alkynes and their derivatives.

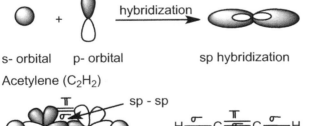

s- orbital   p- orbital   sp hybridization

Acetylene (C_2H_2)

σ = sigma bond; π = pi bond

Determination of hybridization:
Hybridization (X) = Number of sigma bonds + number of lone pairs
2 = sp
3 = sp²
4 = sp³
5 = sp³d
6 = sp³d²
7 = sp³d³
Calculation of number of sigma (σ) bonds:
CH_4 = 4 σ bonds
Atom – Valency
H – 1
O – 2
N – 3
C – 4

$SO_3 \rightarrow$
```
    O
    ||
    S
   / \
  O   O
```
3 sigma bonds,

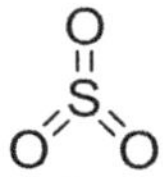

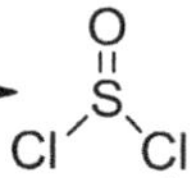

$CO_2 \rightarrow$ O=C=O
2 sigma bonds,

$SOCl_2 \rightarrow$
```
    O
    ||
    S
   / \
  Cl  Cl
```
3 sigma onds

Calculation of number of lone pairs:
Non-bonding electrons = [Group number in periodic table] – [Number of bonds formed (σ + π)]
Non bonding electrons:
NH_3 = 5 [Group number] – 3 [Number of bonds] = 2 (i.e. one lone pair electrons)
H_2O = 6 – 2 = 4 (i.e. two lone pair electrons)
CH_4 = 4 – 4 = 0 (no lone pair electrons)
SO_3 = 6 – 6 = 0
CO_2 = 4 – 4 = 0
$SO2$ = 6 – 4 = 2 (one lone pair electrons)
Hybridization (X):

1. CH_4: $X = 4\sigma + 0$ (zero lone pair electrons)
   $X = 4 = sp^3$
2. BF_3: $X = 3\sigma + 0$ (zero lone pair electrons) $= 3 = sp^2$
3. CO_2: $X = 2\sigma + 0$ (zero lone pair electrons) $= 2 = sp$
4. NH_3 : $X = 3\sigma + 1$ (one lone pair) $= 4 = sp^3$
5. SO_3: $X = 3\sigma + 0$ (zero lone pair) $= 3 = sp^2$
6. SO_2: $X = 2\sigma + 1$ (one lone pair) $= 3 = sp^2$
7. $SOCl_2$: $X = 3\sigma + 1$ (one lone pair) $= 4 = sp^3$
8. $COCl_2$: $X = 3\sigma + 0$ (zero lone pair) $= 3 = sp^2$
9. $^+CH_3$: $X = 3\sigma + 0$ (zero lone pair) $= 3 = sp^2$

   no. of lone pair of electrons
   $= 4$ (gp no. in periodic table) - 3 (no. of bonds)
   $= 1$ (only one electron, i.e. zero pair)

10. $^\cdot CH_3$: $X = 3\sigma + 0$ (zero lone pair) $= 3 = sp^2$
11. $^-CH_3$: $X = 3\sigma + 1$ (one lone pair) $= 4 = sp^3$
12. H_3O^+ : number of lone pair electrons $= 6$ (gp no. in periodic table) $- 3$ (no. of bonds) $= 3$ (one pair)
    Therefore $X = 3\sigma + 1$ (one lone pair) $= 4 = sp^3$
13. $^+NH_4$: number of lone pair electrons $= 5$ (gp no. in periodic table) $- 4$ (no. of bonds) $= 1$ (zero pair)
    Therefore $X = 4\sigma + 0$ (zero lone pair) $= 4 = sp^3$
14. CO : number of lone pair electrons $= 4$ [gp no. in periodic table] $- 3$ [no. of bonds ($\sigma + \pi$)] $= 1$ (zero pair)

    $C \equiv O$ $X = 1\sigma + 1$ (negative charge on carbon) $= 2 = sp$
15. PCl_5: $X = 5\sigma + 0$ (zero lone pair) $= 5 = sp^3d$
16. SF_6: $X = 6\sigma + 0$ (zero lone pair) $= 6 = sp^3d^2$
17. IF_7: $X = 7\sigma + 0$ (zero lone pair) $= 7 = sp^3d^3$
18. What is the hybridization of middle carbon of allene?
    Allene (propadiene): $H_2C = C = CH_2$
    $X = 2\sigma + 0$ (zero lone pair) $= 2 = sp$
19.

$$\underset{sp^2}{\overset{sp^3}{H_3C}}-\underset{H}{\overset{sp^2}{C}}=\underset{H}{\overset{sp}{C}}-\underset{}{\overset{sp}{C}}\equiv\underset{sp}{C}-\underset{sp^2}{\overset{sp}{C}}=\underset{sp^2}{\overset{sp}{C}}=\underset{}{\overset{sp^3}{C}}-CH_3$$

20. Acetyleacetone

    Acetyleacetone

$$\underset{sp^3\ sp^2\ sp^3\ sp^2\ sp^2}{H_3C-\overset{O}{\overset{\|}{C}}-\overset{H_2}{C}-\overset{O}{\overset{\|}{C}}-CH_3} \quad \begin{array}{l} sp^3 : sp^2 \\ 3 : 2 \end{array}$$

21.

$$\underset{sp^3\ sp^2\ sp^3\ sp^2\ sp^2\ sp^3}{H_3C-\overset{O}{\overset{\|}{C}}-\overset{H_2}{C}-\overset{H_2}{C}-\overset{O}{\overset{\|}{C}}-CH_3} \quad \begin{array}{l} sp^3 : sp^2 \\ 4 : 2 \\ 2 : 1 \end{array}$$

22.

[Hexamethylbenzene structure with H$_3$C groups at all six positions]

$sp^3 : sp^2$
$6 : 6$
$1 : 1$

23. Tropylium ion: all are sp²

    Tropylium ion: all are sp2

    [Two resonance structures of tropylium cation]

24. In an organic compound 'x' having molecular formula C$_4$H$_8$ with all sp3 hybridized carbons.

H₂C–CH₂
| |
H₂C–CH₂
cyclobutane

25. In an organic compound 'x' molecular formula having C_4H_6 in which all the three types of sp, sp^2, sp^3 hybridization is found.

$$H_3C-\underset{sp^3}{C}(=O)-\underset{sp^2}{C}\equiv \underset{sp^3}{C}-\underset{sp^2}{C}(=O)-\underset{sp^2}{CH_3}$$ (with H_2 shown)

26. C_4H_4 in which sp and sp^2 hybridization in 1:1 ratio.
    Two isomers are possible

    $H_2C=C=C=CH_2$ $HC\equiv C-C=CH_2$
    sp^2 sp   sp sp^2 sp sp sp^2 sp^2 (with H)

27. Further examples:
    1. CO_2 and CO
       CO_2 = sp and CO = sp
    2. NH_3 and $^+NH_4$
       NH_3 = sp^3 and $^+NH_4$ = sp^3
    3. SO_3 and H_2SO_3
       SO_3 = sp^2 but H_2SO_3 = sp^3
    4. H_2O and H_3O^+
       H_2O = sp^3 and H_3O^+ = sp^3
    5. CO_2 and SO_2
       CO_2 = sp but SO_2 = sp^2
    6. $CHCl_3$ and CH_3Cl
       $CHCl_3$ = sp^3 and CH_3Cl = sp^3
    7. H_2SO_4 and H_2SO_3
       H_2SO_4 = sp^3 and H_2SO_3 = sp^3
    8. CO_3^{-2} and HCO_3^{-1}
       CO_3^{-2} = sp^2 and HCO_3^{-1} = sp^2
    9. $COCl_2$ and $SOCl_2$
       $COCl_2$ = sp^2 but $SOCl_2$ = sp^3

10. SO_3^{-2} and CO_3^{-2}
SO_3^{-2} = sp³ but CO_3^{-2} = sp²
11. CH_4O and CH_2O
CH_4O = sp³ but CH_2O = sp²
12. $^+CH_3$ and $^-CH_3$
$^+CH_3$ = sp² but $^-CH_3$ = sp³

Parameters of Molecular Structure

1. Bond Lengths
2. Bond Angles
3. Bond Energies

1.2. Bond Lengths: Average distance between centers of two bonded atoms.
Factors affecting on bond lengths:
a. Hybridization
b. Electro negativity
c. De-localization

a. Effects of Hybridization:
C — C Single bond sp³ bond length = 1.54 °A (one Angstrom = 10^{-10} meters)
C = C Double bond sp² bond length = 1.34 °A
C ≡ C Triple bond sp bond length = 1.21 °A
For example: C, N bond lengths are sp³ > sp² > sp (i > ii > iii)

i. H_3C-NH_2 ii. $H_2C=NH$ iii. HC≡N
   ↑   ↑   ↑   ↑   ↑ ↑
 sp³ sp³   sp² sp²   sp sp

b. Electronegativity effect:
If electronegativity more bond length will be less.
i.   In a group as electronegativity decreases from top to bottom the bond length increases.

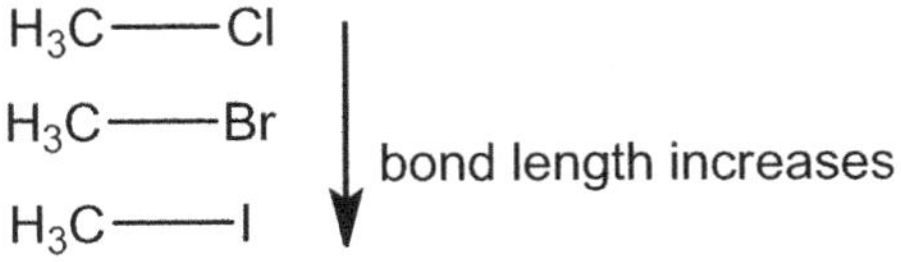

H_3C——Cl
H_3C——Br ⟶ bond length increases
H_3C——I

ii. In a period as electronegativity increases from left to right the bond length decreases.

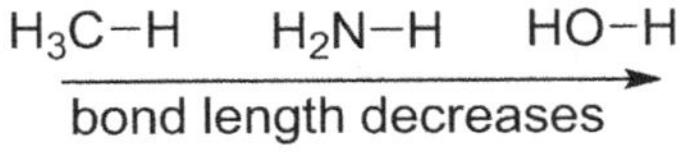

H_3C-H H_2N-H $HO-H$
⎯⎯⎯⎯⎯⎯⎯⎯⎯⎯⎯⎯⟶
bond length decreases

c. De-localization:
i. Resonance
ii. Hyperconjugation

i. Resonance: When two multiple bonds in conjugation then resonance possible or one multiple bond and another lone pair is essential for resonance.

For example: I. ethyl chloride and II. vinyl chloride

I. Ethyl chloride

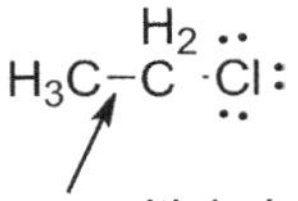

$$H_3C-\overset{H_2}{C}-\overset{..}{\underset{..}{Cl}}:$$

No. of alpha - multiple bonds
No. conjugation

II. vinyl chloride

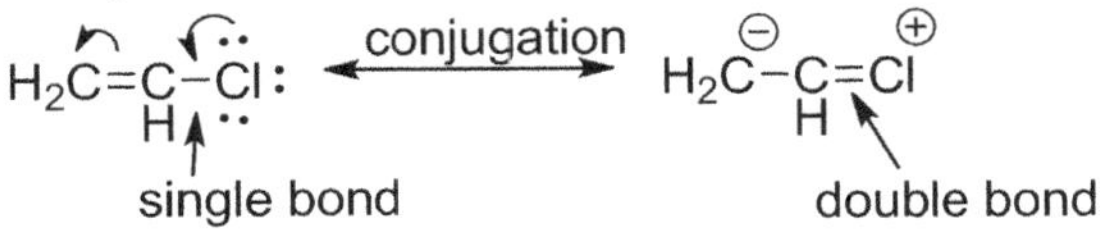

$H_2C=\overset{..}{\underset{H}{C}}-\overset{..}{\underset{..}{Cl}}:$ ⇌ conjugation ⇌ $H_2\overset{\ominus}{C}-\underset{H}{C}=\overset{\oplus}{Cl}$

single bond   double bond

C – Cl bond length in vinyl chloride is less than ethyl chloride because of resonance (I > II).

III. Acrolene and IV. Formaldehyde

III. acrolene

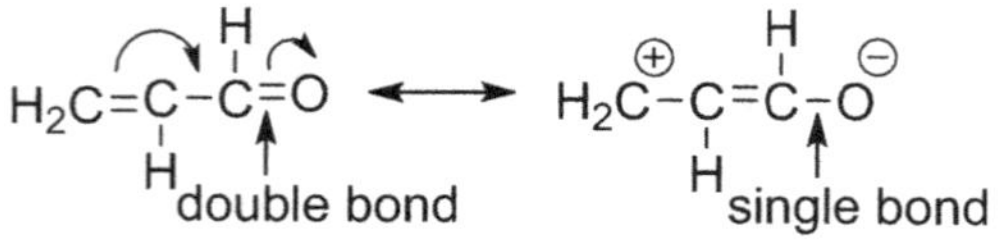

$$H_2C=CH-CHO \longleftrightarrow H_2\overset{\oplus}{C}-CH=CH-\overset{\ominus}{O}$$

　　　double bond　　　　　　single bond

IV. formaldehyde

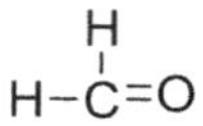

$$H-CHO$$

C – O bond length in acrolene is greater than formaldehyde (III > IV).

V. Benzyl bromide and VI. Bromobenzene

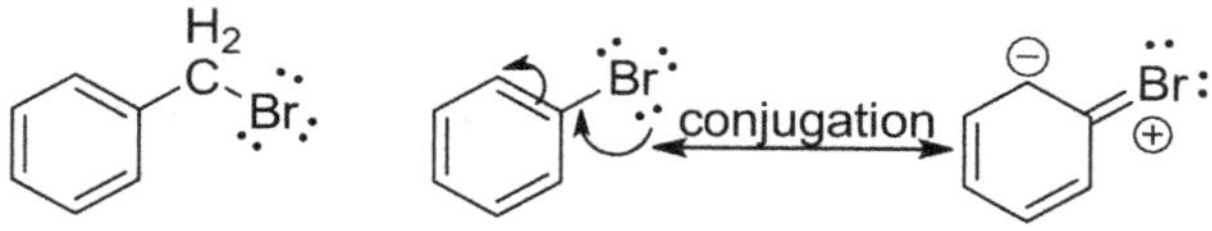

V. Benzyl bromide　　　VI. Bromobenzene (conjugation)

C – Br bond length in benzyl bromide is greater than bromobenzene (V > VI).

VI. $H_2C=CH-CH_2-\ddot{N}H_2$　　　VII. $H_3C-CH=CH-\ddot{N}H_2$

C – N bond length in compound VII is less than VI (VI > VII).

ii. Hyperconjugation:

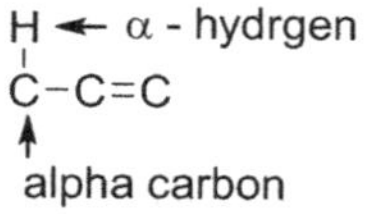

$$\underset{\uparrow}{\underset{\text{alpha carbon}}{C}}(\text{H} \leftarrow \alpha\text{-hydrgen})-C=C$$

For example:

a. Formaldehyde and acetaldehyde

I. formaldehyde

H
|
H−C=O
  ↑
double bond

II. acetaldehyde

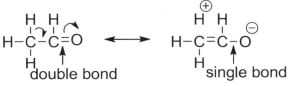

C = O bond length in acetaldehyde is greater than formaldehyde (II > I).

b. tButyl cyanide and methyl cyanide.

I. tertButyl cyanide

CH₃
|
H₃C−C−C≡N
|
CH₃

No. of alpha hydrogens
No hyperconjugation

II. methyl cyanide

H
|
H−C−C≡N ⇌ hyper-conjugation ⇌ H−C=C=N
|
H

three alpha hydrogens, triple bond → double bond

C≡N bond length in methyl cyanide is greater than tert-Butyl cyanide (II > I).

c. If hyperconjugation is not possible then it can be explained by resonance.

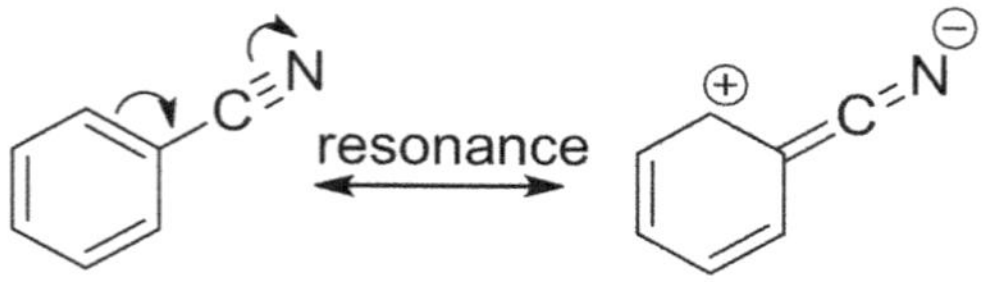

[Structures showing resonance of cyanobenzene]

I. cyano benzene

$$H-C\equiv N$$

II. hydrogen cyanide

$C\equiv N$ bond length in cyanobenzene is greater than hydrogen cyanide (I > II).

1.3. Bond angles: The average angle between the directions of two bonds.

Factors effecting the bond angles are: a. Hybridization; b. Lone pair electrons

a. Hybridization:

Hybridization	Molecular shape	Bond angle
sp^3	Tetrahedral	109° 28'
sp^2	Trigonal planar	120°
sp	Linear	180°

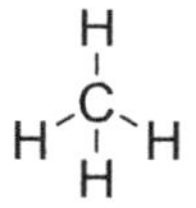

[Structure of methane with H-C-H bonds]

methane = sp^3 hybridization
shape = tetrahedral
bond angle = 109° 28'

b. Lone pair electrons:

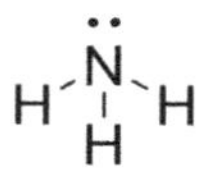

[Structure of NH₃]

i. NH_3 = sp^3 hybridization
shape = trigonal pyramidal
bond angle = 107°

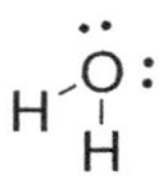

[Structure of H₂O]

ii. H_2O = sp^3 hybridization
shape = bent or angular
bond angle = 104.5°

NH_3 - sp^3 – expected bond angle - 109° 28', but due to lone pair electrons and single bond repulsion the bond angle is 107° and the shape is Trigonal pyramidal.

H_2O - sp^3 – because of repulsion of lone pair electrons the bond angle is 104.5° and the shape is bent or angular.

Bond angles:

$\overset{+}{C}H_3$ - sp^2 - 120°

CH_4 - sp^3 - 109° 28'

$:\overset{-}{C}H_3$ - sp^3 - 107°

$:\overset{-}{N}H_2$ - sp^3 - 104.5°

$H_3\overset{+}{O}:$ - sp^3 - 107°

$\overset{+}{N}H_4:$ - sp^3 - 109° 28'

1.4. Bond energies: The amount of energy required to break a bond or to form a bond is called bond energy. Factors effecting bond energies are: i. bond length; ii. Lone pair of electrons.

i. Bond length: In general bond length is inversely proportional to bond energy.

$$\text{bond length (proportional to)} = \frac{1}{\text{bond energy}}$$

bond length decreases ↓ ↓ bond energy increases

—C–C— ~ 81 kcal/mole

—C=C— ~146 kcal/mole

—C≡C— ~192 kcal/mole

ii. Lone pair of electrons:

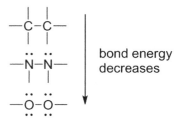

bond energy decreases

Bond energy decreases because of repulsion between lone pair of electrons and adjacent atoms.

$$R-O^- + BrH \longrightarrow R-O-H + Br^-$$
$$\xcancel{\longrightarrow} R-O-Br: + H^+$$

it is not formed due to repulsion of lone pair electron

Shapes of molecules:

sp³: 4 sigma - tetrahedral - AB₄ - example CH₄

3 sigma + 1 lone pair - pyramidal - AB₃ - example NH₃

2 sigma + 2 lone pairs - angular or 'V' shape - AB₂ - example H₂O

sp²: 3 sigma - trigonal planar - AB₃

2 sigma + 1 lone pair - angular or 'V' shape

sp²: 2 sigma - linear - AB₂   B−A−B

Examples:
1. SO₃   - sp² – Trigonal planar
2. H₃O⁺ - sp³ – Pyramidal
3. COCl₂ - sp² – Trigonal planar

4. C_2H_2 - sp – Linear
5. SO_2 - sp^2 – Angular
6. H_2N^- - sp^3 – Angular
7. H_3C^- - sp^3 – pyramidal
8. $CHCl_3$ - sp^3 – Tetrahedral
9. $H_3C \cdot$ - sp^2 – Trigonal planar
10. CH_2O - sp^2 – Trigonal planar
11. Linear molecule or molecules among following
    a) C_2H_2 b) C_2HCH_3 c) both d) C_2H_4 e) all
    Answer: a) C_2H_2
    H−C≡C−C≡C−H   linear

    $\begin{array}{cc} H & H \\ \diagdown & \diagup \\ C=C \\ \diagup & \diagdown \\ H & H \end{array}$ non-linear

12. Planar molecule or molecules among the following
    a) C_2H_4 b) C_2H_2 c) both d) C_3H_6 e) all
    Answer: c) both
    All linear molecules are planar.

    sp - planar
    sp^2 - planar
    sp, sp^2 - both present - planar
    all are planar except sp^3

13. Toluene, styrene

    $sp^3 \longrightarrow CH_3$ $HC=CH_2$

    Toluene   Styrene
    sp^3 - no-planar   no sp^3 - planar

14. CH_2CHCCH
    $H_2C=\underset{H}{C}-C\equiv CH$ planar

15. Allene: non linear because when ever the two double bonds are continuous then they will be perpendicular to each other hence they will not be linear.
$H_2C=C=CH_2$
allene - non-linear
16. One 'Carbon' with sp
i. $HC\equiv N$ ii. $O=C=O$
17. One 'Carbon' with sp^2

i. $H-\underset{\underset{H}{\|}}{\overset{O}{\|}}$ ii. $Cl-\underset{\underset{Cl}{\|}}{\overset{O}{\|}}$ iii. $H-\underset{\underset{NH_2}{\|}}{\overset{O}{\|}}$

iv. $H-\underset{\underset{Cl}{\|}}{\overset{O}{\|}}$ v. $H-\underset{\underset{OH}{\|}}{\overset{O}{\|}}$ vi. $\overset{\oplus}{C}H_3$ vii. $\dot{C}H_3$

2. Reactivity of Organic Molecules

Reaction: Reactant + Reagent → Product + Byproduct
Equation: R – X + HO⁻ → R – OH + X⁻

Reaction Mechanism: 1. Bond Fission; 2. Types of Reagents; 3. Types of Reaction

2.1. Bond Fission

(i) Homolytic fission; (ii) Heterolytic fission

i. Homolytic fission: Symmetrical cleavage of bond is known as hemolytic fission. It is represented with fish hook (⌒) arrow mark.

$$A\!-\!A \longrightarrow \underbrace{\dot{A}-\dot{A}}_{\text{free radicals}}$$

When two bonded atoms are merely same electronegativity then heterolytic fission takes place.

$$Cl\!-\!Cl \longrightarrow 2\dot{C}l$$

Between carbon and hydrogen the electronegativity difference is very less so hemolytic fission takes place.

$$-\!\overset{|}{\underset{|}{C}}\!-\!H \longrightarrow -\!\overset{|}{\underset{|}{\dot{C}}} + \dot{H}$$

If homolytic fission takes place radically it is called radical mechanism.

ii. Heterolytic fission: Unsymmetrical cleavage of a bond is known as heterolytic fission. It is represented with arrow (⌒) mark and the arrow mark shown towards more electronegative molecules.

$$A\!-\!B \longrightarrow \underbrace{\overset{\oplus}{A} + \overset{\ominus}{B}}_{\text{cation + anion}}$$

ions are formed

Electronegativity difference is very large then only heterolytic fission takes place.

For example: (i) $R\overset{\frown}{-}Cl$ (ii) $H\overset{\frown}{-}Cl$ (iii) $C\overset{\frown}{=}O$ (iv) $H\overset{\frown}{-}Br$

Ionic mechanism: Ions reacts with ions only.
Radical mechanism: Radicals reacts with radicals only.

2.2. Types of reagents

$Ph - CH_2 - Cl + Reagent \rightarrow Product + Byproduct$

(i) Free radical reagents (free radicals)
(ii) Electrophilic reagents (Electrophiles)
(iii) Nucleophilic reagents (Nucleophiles)

i. Free radical reagents: Free radicals are odd electronic species with odd number of electrons. These are formed by homolytic fission.

For example: $\overset{.}{H}$ (hydro free radicals), $\overset{.}{Cl}, \overset{.}{Br}, \overset{.}{I}$,

$\overset{.}{O}H, \overset{.}{O}R, \overset{.}{N}O_2$

$\overset{.}{R} \rightarrow (\overset{.}{C}H_3, H_3C-\overset{.}{C}H_2$, etc.)

$\overset{.}{P}h$ (Phenyl radical), $Ph-\overset{.}{C}H_2, H_2C=HC-\overset{.}{C}H_2$, etc.

Total number of electrons will be odd number:

$\overset{.}{N}O_2 = 7 + 16 = 23$.

ii. Electrophilic reagents (Electrophiles): These are electron deficiency species (or) electron seeking (or) electron loving species (or) electron pair accepting species.

For example: BF_3, carbenes, all cations, Lewis acids.

(a) Positive electrophiles: Positively charged.
(b) Neutral electrophiles: Neutrally charged
(a) Positive electrophiles: All cations.

For example: $\overset{\oplus}{H}$, $\overset{\oplus}{NO_2}$, $\overset{\oplus}{R}$, $R-\overset{\oplus}{C}=O$, $\overset{\oplus}{Cl}$, $\overset{\oplus}{Br}$, $Ph\overset{\oplus}{N_2}$, etc.

(b) Neutral electrophiles: These are neutral in nature.

For example: BF_3, $AlCl_3$, $FeCl_3$, $ZnCl_2$, $\overset{..}{C}Cl_2$ (dichloro carbene), $\overset{..}{C}HCl$ (mono-chloro carbene), $\overset{..}{C}HBr$, $\overset{..}{C}H_2$, $\overset{..}{C}Br_2$, $\overset{..}{C}HBr$,

*SO_3 — net charge is neutral but it acts as electrophile

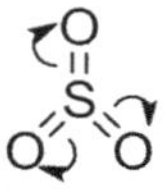

*CO_2 $O=C=O$ O: δ -ve it acts as neutral
C: δ +ve electrophile

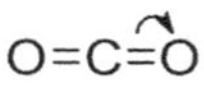

*ICl, O_3, etc.

iii. **Nucleophilic reagents** (Nucleophiles): Electron excess species (or) nucleus loving species (which are negative charged) (or) electron pair donors.
    (a) –ve nucleophiles
    (b) Neutral nucleophiles

(a) –ve Nucleophiles: All anions.

For example: $\overset{\ominus}{H}$, $\overset{\ominus}{Cl}$, $\overset{\ominus}{Br}$, $\overset{\ominus}{I}$, $\overset{\ominus}{OH}$, $\overset{\ominus}{OR}$, $\overset{\ominus}{NH_2}$, $\overset{\ominus}{R}$, $\overset{\ominus}{SR}$, $\overset{\ominus}{CN}$, SO_4^{2-}, $\overset{\ominus}{HSO_3}$, CO_3^{2-}, $\overset{\ominus}{HCO_3}$, SO_3^{2-}, $RC\overset{\ominus}{OO}$, $Ar\overset{\ominus}{O}$

(b) Neutral Nucleophiles: Lewis bases such as:

$\overset{..}{N}H_3$, $R\overset{..}{N}H_2$, $R_2\overset{..}{N}H$, $R_3\overset{..}{N}$, $H_2\overset{..}{N}-\overset{..}{N}H_2$, $PhH\overset{..}{N}-\overset{..}{N}H_2$, $H_2\overset{..}{N}-OH$, $NH_2CONH\overset{..}{N}H_2$, $H_2\overset{..}{\underset{..}{O}}$,

$\overset{..}{R\overset{..}{O}H}$, $R-\overset{..}{\underset{..}{O}}-R$, $R\overset{..}{\underset{..}{S}}H$, $R-\overset{..}{\underset{..}{S}}-R$, $\overset{\ominus\;\oplus}{RMgX}$, RLi, RNa, $RZnBr$

(All organo metal compounds are mostly nucleophiles). (– ium $\oplus$; - ide $\ominus$).

Examples:

1. Bromonium ion → $\overset{\oplus}{Br}$ → +ve Electrophile
2. Methoxide ion → $CH_3\overset{..}{O}^-$ → -ve Neucleophile
3. Aniline → $Ph\overset{..}{N}H_2$ → neutral Neucleophile
4. $\overset{..}{C}HBr$ → neutral Electrophile
5. Aryl diazonium → $Ph-\overset{+}{N}\equiv N$ → +ve Electrophile
6. Deuterium → $\overset{.}{D}$ → free radical
7. $CH_3CH_2CH_2CH_2Li$ → neutral Neucleophile
8. $Ph-C\equiv\overset{\oplus}{O}$ → +ve Electrophile
9. Lithium aluminum hydride → $LiAlH_4$ → neutral Neucleophile
10. Bisulfite ion → HSO_3^- → -ve Neucleophile
11. Hydronium ion → $H_3\overset{\oplus}{O}$ → +ve Electrophile
12.

2.3. Types of Reaction

Types of reactions are broadly classified into 5 types: (I) Substitution (II) Addition (III) Elimination (IV) Molecular Rearrangement reaction (V) Pericyclic reaction.

i. Substitution reaction: 3 types

$$R-X + Y \longrightarrow R-Y + X$$

Based on reagent involved in the substitution reaction it is further classified into 3 types:
(1) Free radical substitution reaction
(2) Electrophilic substitution reaction
(3) Nucleophilic substitution reaction.

ii. Addition reaction: 3 types

$$\underset{/}{\overset{\backslash}{C}}=\underset{\backslash}{\overset{/}{C}} + A-B \longrightarrow -\underset{A}{\overset{\backslash}{C}}-\underset{B}{\overset{/}{C}}-$$

(1) Free radical addition reaction
(2) Electrophilic addition reaction
(3) Nucleophilic addition reaction.

iii. Elimination reaction: 2 types

$$-\underset{A}{\overset{\backslash}{C}}-\underset{B}{\overset{/}{C}}- \longrightarrow \underset{/}{\overset{\backslash}{C}}=\underset{\backslash}{\overset{/}{C}} + A-B$$

(1) α - Elimination
(2) β - Elimination

iv. Molecular Rearrangement reaction: in which rearrangement takes place.

$$\overset{R}{\underset{}{A-B}} \longrightarrow \overset{R}{\underset{}{A-B}}$$

v. Pericyclic reaction.

2.4. Substitution reaction

(1) Free radical substitution reaction:

$$CH_4 + Cl_2 \xrightarrow{h\nu} CH_3Cl + HCl$$

Mechanism: (a) initiation (b) propagation (c) termination.

(a) Initiation:

$$Cl-Cl \longrightarrow 2\dot{C}l$$

(b) Propagation:

$$H-\overset{H}{\underset{H}{C}}-H + \dot{C}l \longrightarrow \dot{C}H_3 + HCl$$

$$\dot{C}H_3 + Cl-Cl \longrightarrow CH_3Cl + \dot{C}l$$

} chain reaction

(c) Termination:

$$\dot{C}H_3 + \dot{C}l \longrightarrow CH_3Cl$$
$$\dot{C}l + \dot{C}l \longrightarrow Cl_2$$
$$\dot{C}H_3 + \dot{C}H_3 \longrightarrow H_3C-CH_3$$

(2) **Electrophilic substitution reaction: Aromatic compounds**

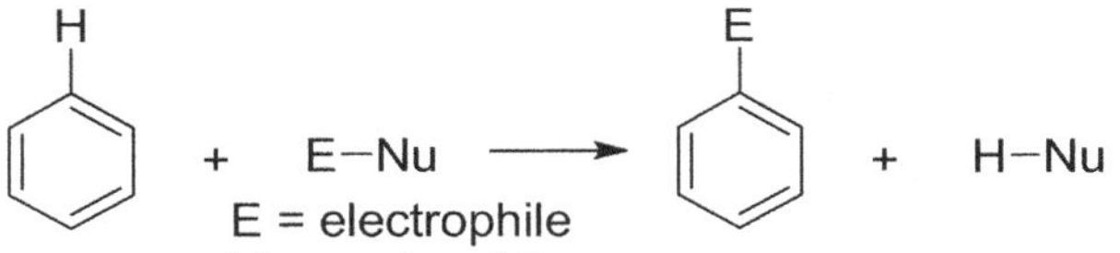

$$C_6H_6 + E-Nu \longrightarrow C_6H_5-E + H-Nu$$

E = electrophile
N = nucleophile

Mechanism: (a) formation of electrophile (b) formation of sigma (σ) complex intermediate (c) removal of $\overset{\oplus}{H}$

(a) Formation of electrophile:

$$E-Nu \rightleftharpoons \overset{\oplus}{E} + \overset{\ominus}{Nu}$$

electrophile   nucleophile

(b) Formation of sigma (σ) complex intermediate (slowest step):

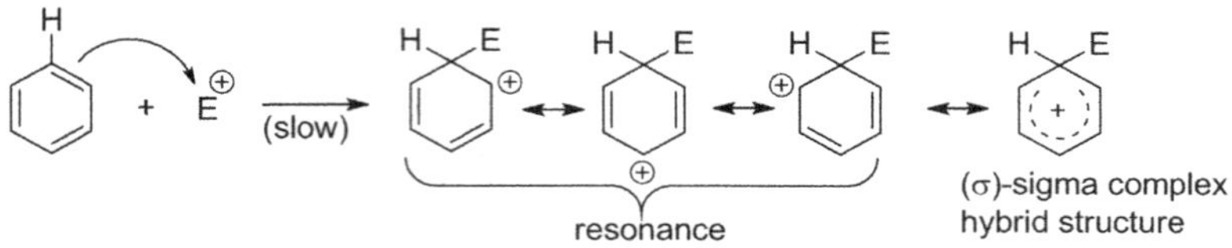

[Diagram: benzene + E⁺ (slow) → sigma complex resonance structures → (σ)-sigma complex hybrid structure]

(c) Removal of $\overset{+}{H}$:

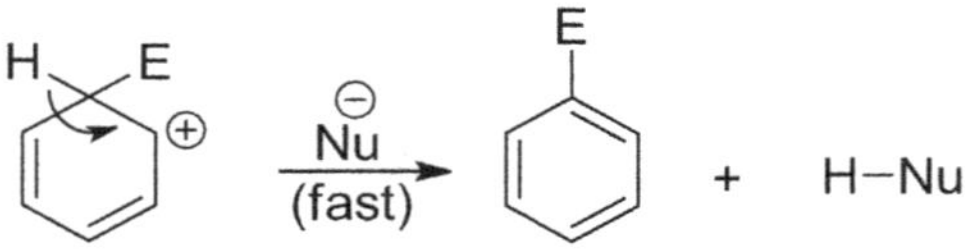

[Diagram: sigma complex + Nu⁻ (fast) → substituted benzene + H–Nu]

Slowest step is rate determining step. Rate of the reaction is proportional to two species so, it is a bimolecular SE^2 reaction (Bimolecular Electrophilic Substitution reaction).

Rate of reaction α [Concentration of benzene (Ph) and electrophile ($\overset{+}{E}$)]

For example:

(i) Nitration:

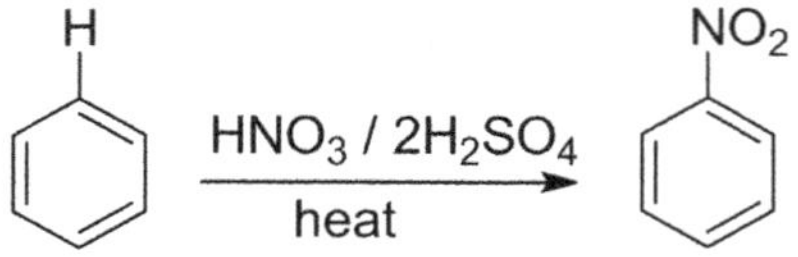

$$C_6H_6 \xrightarrow{HNO_3 / 2H_2SO_4, \text{ heat}} C_6H_5NO_2$$

Mechanism: (a) formation of electrophile ($\overset{+}{NO_2}$)

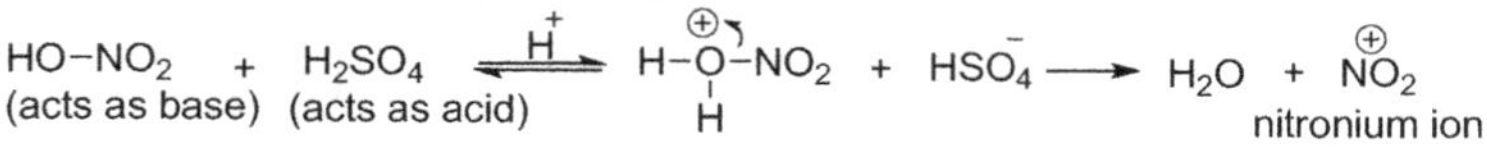

$$HO-NO_2 + H_2SO_4 \rightleftharpoons H-\overset{+}{\underset{H}{O}}-NO_2 + HSO_4^- \longrightarrow H_2O + \overset{+}{NO_2}$$
(acts as base) (acts as acid)   nitronium ion

$$H_2O + H_2SO_4 \rightleftharpoons H_3\overset{+}{O} + HSO_4^-$$

$$HNO_3 + 2H_2SO_4 \rightleftharpoons \overset{\oplus}{N}O_2 + H_3\overset{\oplus}{O} + 2HSO_4^{\ominus}$$

If we take only HNO_3 in reaction then the mechanism will follow as below:

$$HO-NO_2 + HNO_3 \rightleftharpoons H-\overset{\overset{\oplus}{O}}{\underset{H}{-}}NO_2 + NO_2^{\ominus} \longrightarrow H_2O + \overset{\oplus}{N}O_2$$

Structure of

$$\overset{\oplus}{N}O_2 \xleftarrow{\text{structure}} \overset{\oplus}{O=N=O} \longleftrightarrow \overset{\oplus\oplus}{O=N}-\overset{\ominus}{O}$$

(b) Formation of sigma complex:

[benzene + $\overset{\oplus}{N}O_2$ → sigma complex with H and NO_2, ring with $\oplus$]

(c) Removal of $\overset{\oplus}{H}$:

[sigma complex $\xrightarrow[\text{(fast)}]{HSO_4^{\ominus}}$ nitrobenzene + H_2SO_4]

Rate α [benzene] [NO_2] → SE^2 reaction.

[benzene $\xrightarrow{HNO_3 / H_2SO_4}$ nitrobenzene]

[deuterated benzene $\xrightarrow{HNO_3 / H_2SO_4}$ deuterated nitrobenzene]
(D = deuterium)

Rate of the both the reactions are same. There is no isotopic effect (Deuterium) on nitration of benzene

Nitration of mesitylene:

$$\text{mesitylene} \xrightarrow[H_2SO_4]{HNO_3} [\sigma\text{-complex intermediates}] \longrightarrow \text{nitromesitylene} + H^+$$

(ii)   Friedel-Crafts alkylation:

$$C_6H_6 + R-Cl \xrightarrow{AlCl_3} C_6H_5-R$$

Mechanism: (a) formation of electrophile:

a. $R-Cl + AlCl_3 \rightleftharpoons R^+ + AlCl_4^-$

(b) Formation of 'σ' complex:

$$C_6H_6 + R^+ \longrightarrow [C_6H_6R]^+$$

(c) Removal of $\overset{+}{H}$:

$$[C_6H_6R]^+ \xrightarrow{AlCl_4^-} C_6H_5-R + AlCl_3 + HCl$$

(iii)   Friedel-Crafts acylation:

$$C_6H_6 + R-\overset{O}{\underset{\|}{C}}-Cl \xrightarrow{AlCl_3} C_6H_5-\overset{O}{\underset{\|}{C}}-R$$

Mechanism: (a) formation of electrophile

$$R-\overset{O}{\underset{\|}{C}}-Cl + AlCl_3 \rightleftharpoons R-\overset{+}{C}=\overset{..}{\underset{..}{O}} \leftrightarrow R-\overset{O^-}{\underset{\|\|}{C}} \;+\; AlCl_4^-$$

(b) Formation of 'σ' complex:

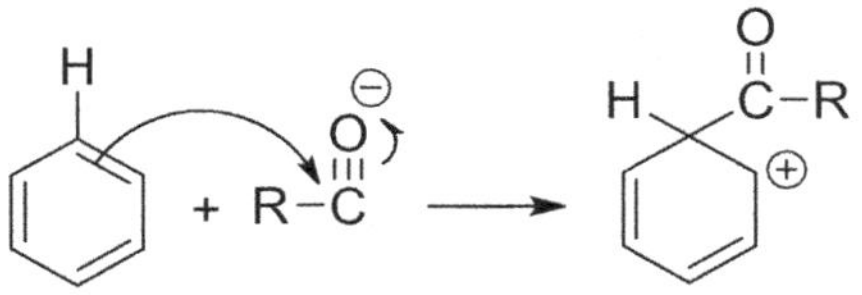

[benzene] + R–C(=O)⁺ ⟶ [cyclohexadienyl cation with H and C(=O)–R substituent]

(c) Removal of H⁺ :

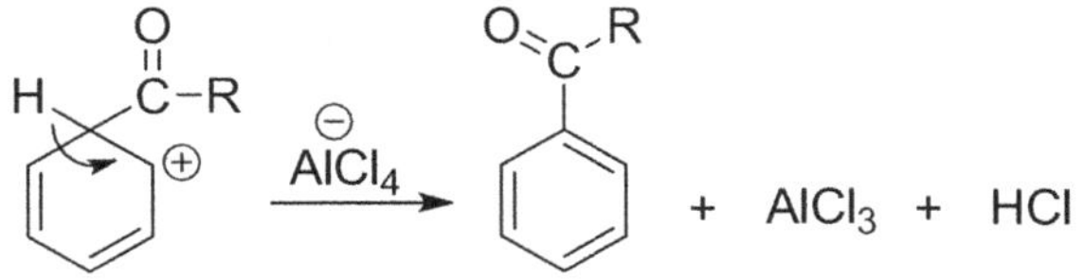

[σ-complex] $\xrightarrow{AlCl_4^-}$ [Ph–C(=O)–R] + AlCl₃ + HCl

(iv) Halogenation:

[benzene] + Cl₂ $\xrightarrow{FeCl_3}$ [chlorobenzene]

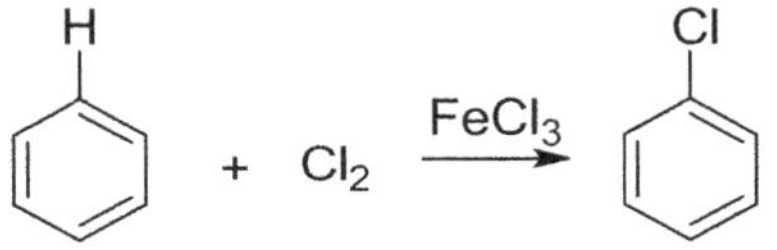

Mechanism: (a) Formation of electrophile:

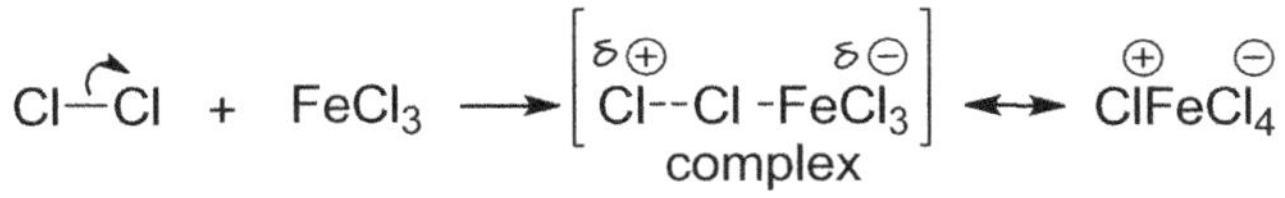

$$Cl-Cl + FeCl_3 \longrightarrow [\overset{\delta+}{Cl}--\overset{\delta-}{Cl}-FeCl_3]_{complex} \longleftrightarrow \overset{+}{Cl}\overset{-}{FeCl_4}$$

(b) Formation of 'σ' complex:

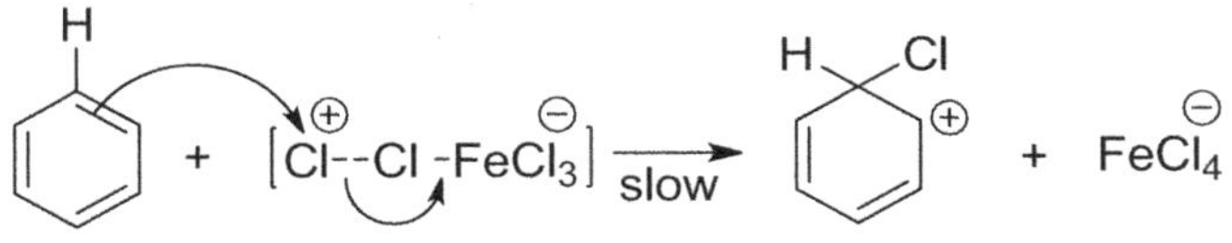

[benzene] + [Cl--Cl-FeCl₃] $\xrightarrow{slow}$ [σ-complex with H and Cl] + FeCl₄⁻

(c) Removal of H⁺ :

[σ-complex] $\xrightarrow[fast]{FeCl_4^-}$ [chlorobenzene] + FeCl₃ + HCl

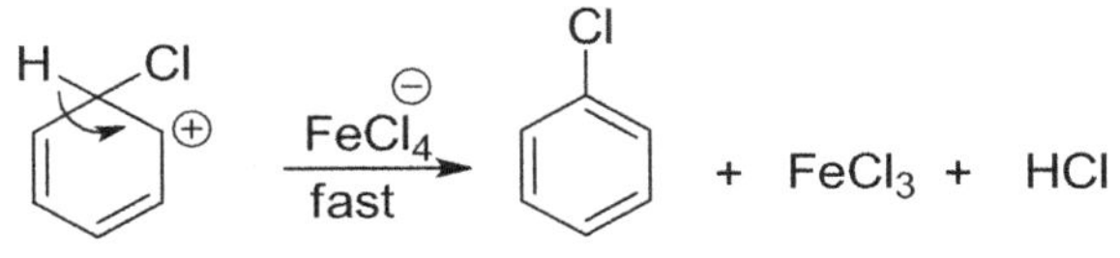

(v) Sulphonation:

31

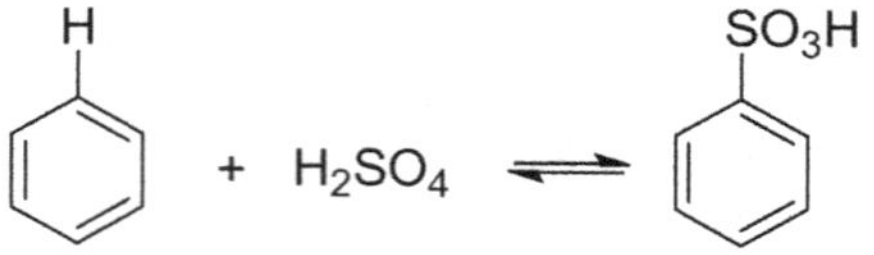

C₆H₆ + H$_2$SO$_4$ ⇌ C₆H₅SO$_3$H

Mechanism: (a) Formation of electrophile

$$H_2SO_4 + H_2SO_4 \rightleftharpoons SO_3^+ + H_3O^+ + HSO_4^-$$
  neutral electrophile

(b) Formation of 'σ' complex:

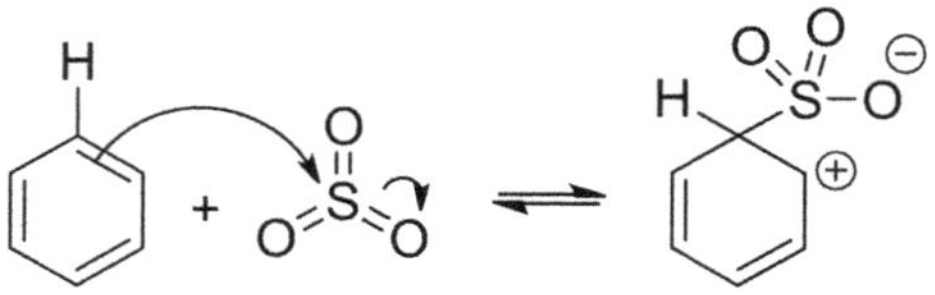

[benzene + SO$_3$ → σ-complex with H and SO$_3^-$]

(c) Removal of H$^+$:

[σ-complex] $\xrightleftharpoons{HSO_4^-}$ [C₆H₅SO$_3^-$] $\xrightarrow{H_3O^+}$ C₆H₅SO$_3$H + H$_2$O + H$_2$SO$_4$

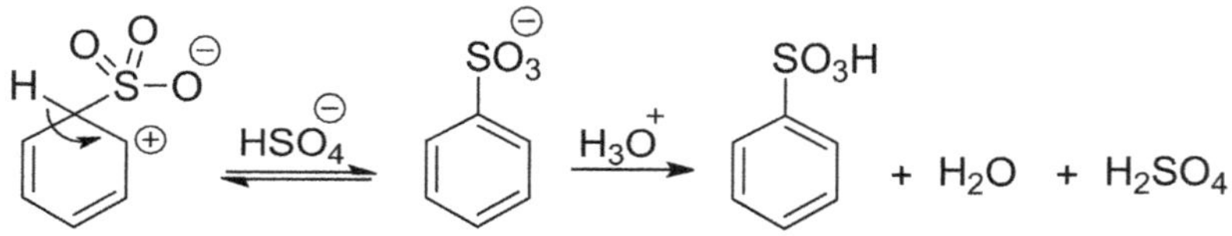

Further examples: a) Sulphonation of toluene

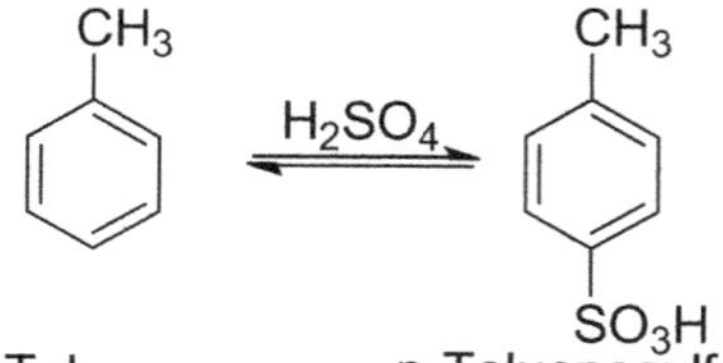

Toluene $\xrightleftharpoons{H_2SO_4}$ p-Toluenesulfonic acid (CH$_3$-C₆H₄-SO$_3$H)

b) Friedel-Crafts acylation of p-xylene:
c)

$$\text{p-xylene} + H_3C-\underset{\underset{}{\overset{O}{\|}}}{C}-Cl \xrightarrow{AlCl_3} \text{2,5-dimethylacetophenone}$$

(3) Nucleophilic substitution reaction:

$$R-X + Y^{\ominus} \longrightarrow R-Y + X^{\ominus}$$

Further classified into 3 types:
(i) Unimolecular Nucleophilic Substitution reaction (SN^1)
(ii) Bimolecular Nucleophilic Substitution reaction (SN^2)
(iii) Intra-molecular Nucleophilic Substitution reaction (SN^i)

(i). Unimolecular Nucleophilic Substitution reaction (SN^1):

$$\underset{\text{chiral-tert-alkyl halide}}{R_2-\underset{R_3}{\overset{R_1}{\underset{|}{\overset{|}{C}}}}-Cl} \xrightarrow{aq.\ KOH} \underset{50\%}{R_2-\underset{R_3}{\overset{R_1}{\underset{|}{\overset{|}{C}}}}-OH} + \underset{50\%}{HO-\underset{R_3}{\overset{R_1}{\underset{|}{\overset{|}{C}}}}-R_2}$$

enantiomers / racemic mixture

Mechanism:

$$R_2-\overset{R_1}{\underset{R_3}{\overset{|}{C}}}\curvearrowright Cl \xrightarrow[\text{slow rate determining step}]{-Cl^{\ominus}} \underset{\text{tert-carbo cation intermediate}}{R_2-\overset{R_1}{\underset{R_3}{\overset{|}{C^{\oplus}}}}} \xrightarrow[\text{fast}]{\overset{aq.\ KOH}{\overline{OH}}} \underset{50\%}{R_2-\overset{R_1}{\underset{R_3}{\overset{|}{C}}}-OH} + \underset{50\%}{H_2O-\overset{R_1}{\underset{R_3}{\overset{|}{C}}}-R_2}$$

Rate of the reaction α [Alkyl halide] → SN^1

It takes place in more than one step. Hence it is called as non-concerted reaction. SN1 takes place tertiary alkyl halides. But no takes place in primary alkyl halides.

(ii). **Bimolecular Nucleophilic Substitution reaction (SN^2):**

$$\underset{\text{chiral primary-alkyl halide}}{\overset{R}{\underset{D}{H-C-Cl}}} \xrightarrow{\text{aq. KOH}} \underset{100\%}{\overset{R}{\underset{D}{HO-C-H}}}$$

Mechanism:

$$\underset{\substack{\text{single step (concerted) reaction}}}{\overset{R}{\underset{D}{H-C-Cl}} \xrightarrow{\overset{\ominus}{OH}} \underset{\text{transition state}}{\left[\overset{R}{\underset{H\ \ D}{HO^{\delta\ominus}-\underset{}{C}---Cl^{\delta\ominus}}}\right]} \longrightarrow \underset{\text{Walden inversion}}{\overset{R}{\underset{D}{HO-C-H}}}}$$

Rate of the reaction α [(alkyl halide) × (OH)] → SN^2 → Bimolecular

If the nucleophile attacks from the opposite side of the leaving nucleophile it known as inversion. It is detected by Walden inversion. SN2 reaction takes place in primary alkyl halide but not in tertiary alkyl halide.

Differences between SN¹ and SN²:

SN¹	SN²
1. Takes place in tertiary alkyl halides	1. Primary alkyl halide
2. Two steps	2. Only one step
3. 1st slow and rate determining step	3. Only one step
4. Rate is α to concentration of alkyl halide	4. Rate is α to concentration of alkyl halide × alkali
5. Unimolecular	5. Bimolecular
6. Non-concerted	6. Concerted
7. Independent of concentration of alkali	7. Dependent on concentration of both
8. Carbo-cation intermediate is formed	8. Takes place via only transition state
9. Racemic mixture is formed provided reactant is chiral	9. Walden inversion takes place provided reactant is chiral
10. Favorable in protic solvents such as water, formic acid	10. Favorable in aprotic solvents such as dimethyl sufoxide, dimethylformamide, etc.
11. Order of reactivity: tertiary > secondary > primary	11. Order of reactivity: primary > secondary > tertiary
12. Rearrangement may takes place	12. No rearrangement takes place

(iii) **Intra-molecular Nucleophilic Substitution reaction (SNⁱ):**

$$\begin{array}{c} R_1 \\ | \\ H-C-OH \\ | \\ R_2 \end{array} \xrightarrow{SOCl_2} \begin{array}{c} R_1 \\ | \\ H-C-Cl \\ | \\ R_2 \end{array}$$

Mechanism:

$$H-\underset{R_2}{\overset{R_1}{C}}-O{\vdots}H + Cl{\vdots}\overset{O}{\underset{\parallel}{S}}-Cl \xrightarrow[-HCl]{} H-\underset{R_2}{\overset{R_1}{C}}-O-\overset{O}{\underset{\parallel}{S}}-Cl \longrightarrow$$

$$H-\underset{R_2}{\overset{R_1}{C}}\underset{Cl}{\overset{O}{\cdots}}S=O \longrightarrow H-\underset{R_2}{\overset{R_1}{C}}-Cl + SO_2$$

Retention product

2.5. Addition reaction

(1). Free radical addition reaction:

$$H_2C=CH_2 + Cl_2 \xrightarrow{h\nu} \underset{Cl\ Cl}{H_2C-CH_2}$$

Mechanism: (a) initiation (b) propagation (c) termination
(a) Initiation:

$$Cl-Cl \longrightarrow 2\ \dot{C}l$$

(b) Propagation:

$$H_2C=CH_2 + \dot{C}l \longrightarrow \underset{Cl}{H_2C-\dot{C}H_2}$$

$$\underset{Cl}{H_2C-\dot{C}H_2} + Cl-Cl \longrightarrow \underset{Cl\ Cl}{H_2C-CH_2} + \dot{C}l$$

} chain reaction

(c) Termination:

$$\underset{Cl}{H_2C-\dot{C}H_2} + \dot{C}l \longrightarrow \underset{Cl\ Cl}{H_2C-CH_2}$$

$$\underset{Cl}{H_2C-\dot{C}H_2} + \underset{Cl}{H_2\dot{C}-CH_2} \longrightarrow \underset{Cl}{H_2C}-\overset{H_2}{\underset{Cl}{C}}-\overset{H_2}{\underset{}{C}}-\underset{Cl}{CH_2}$$

$$\dot{C}l + \dot{C}l \longrightarrow Cl_2$$

(2). Electrophilic addition reaction:
Alkenes:

$$H_2C=CH_2 + HBr \longrightarrow \underset{H\ \ Br}{H_2C-CH_2}$$

Mechanism: Addition reaction first electrophile added and next nucleophile.

$$H_2C=CH_2 + HBr \longrightarrow C_2H_5Br$$

$$H_2C=CH_2 + HBr \xrightarrow{\text{slow}} \underset{\text{carbocation}\ \text{more stable}}{H_2\overset{+}{C}-\underset{H}{CH_2}} \xrightarrow{Br^-} \underset{H\ \ Br}{H_2C-CH_2}$$

$$\underset{\text{carbanion less stable}}{H_2\overset{-}{C}-\underset{Br}{CH_2}}$$ (slow pathway blocked)

It is known that $\overset{+}{C}$ is more stable than $\overset{-}{C}$, i.e. [$\overset{+}{C}$ > $\overset{-}{C}$]

Note: $\overset{-}{O}$, $\overset{-}{N}$, $\overset{-}{F}$ are stable but not $\overset{-}{C}$

Alkenes always undergo electrophilic addition reaction but not nucleophilic addition reaction.

(3). Nucleophilic addition reaction:
Carbonyl compounds:

$$\underset{}{R-\overset{O}{\underset{\|}{C}}-H} + E-Nu \longrightarrow \underset{Nu}{R-\overset{OE}{\underset{|}{C}}-H}$$

Mechanism:

$$R-\overset{\overset{\delta\ominus}{O}}{\underset{\delta\oplus}{C}}-H + E-Nu \xrightarrow{slow} \begin{matrix} \overset{\ominus}{O} \\ R-C-H \\ | \\ Nu \\ \text{(more stable)} \end{matrix} \xrightarrow[fast]{\overset{\oplus}{E}} \begin{matrix} OE \\ | \\ R-C-H \\ | \\ Nu \end{matrix}$$

(with less stable alternative: R–C(OE)–H with ⊕)

Carbonyl compounds always undergo nucleophilic addition reactions.

2.6. Elimination reaction

(1). α – Elimination reaction: If two atoms or groups are removed from same atom is known as α (alpha) - elimination reaction:

$$CHCl_3 \xrightarrow[-HCl]{NaOH} :CCl_2$$

Mechanism:

$$\underset{Cl}{\overset{H}{Cl-\overset{|}{C}-Cl}} \xrightarrow{\overset{\ominus}{OH}} H_2O + \underset{Cl}{\overset{\ominus}{Cl-\overset{|}{C}-Cl}} \xrightarrow{-Cl^{\ominus}} \underset{Cl}{Cl-\overset{..}{C}}$$

(2). β – Elimination reaction: If two atoms or groups are removed from adjacent atoms are called as β (beta) – elimination reaction.

$$-\underset{H}{\overset{|}{C}}-\underset{X}{\overset{|}{C}}- \xrightarrow{-HX} \overset{}{C}=\overset{}{C}$$

Further classified into 3 types:
(i) Unimolecular elimination reaction (E_1)
(ii) Bimolecular elimination reaction (E_2)
(iii) Elimination Unimolecular via conjugate base (E_1cB)

(i). Unimolecular elimination reaction (E_1):

$$\underset{\substack{\text{H Cl}\\ \text{3° Alkyl halide}}}{\overset{\text{R R}}{R-\overset{|}{\underset{|}{C}}-\overset{|}{\underset{|}{C}}-R}} \xrightarrow[-HCl]{\text{alc. KOH}} \overset{\text{R R}}{R-\overset{|}{C}=\overset{|}{C}-R}$$

Mechanism:

$$\underset{\text{H Cl}}{\overset{\text{R R}}{R-\overset{|}{\underset{|}{C}}-\overset{|}{\underset{|}{C}}-R}} \xrightarrow[\substack{\text{slow rate}\\ \text{determining}\\ \text{step}}]{^{\ominus}-Cl} \underset{\substack{\text{H}\\ \text{carbocation}\\ \text{intermediate}}}{\overset{\text{R R}}{R-\overset{|}{C}-\overset{\oplus}{\underset{|}{C}}-R}} \xrightarrow[\substack{^{\ominus}\text{OH}\\ \text{alc. KOH}\\ \text{fast}}]{} \overset{\text{R R}}{R-\overset{|}{C}=\overset{|}{C}-R}$$

Rate α [alkyl halide] → so unimolecular → E_1 → non-concerted reaction
Primary alkyl halide will not take place.

(ii) **Bimolecular elimination reaction (E_2):**

$$\underset{\substack{\text{H H}\\ \text{1° Alkyl halide}}}{\overset{\text{H Cl}}{H-\overset{|}{\underset{|}{C}}-\overset{|}{\underset{|}{C}}-H}} \xrightarrow{\text{alc. KOH}} \underset{\text{H}}{\overset{\text{H}}{H-\overset{|}{C}=\overset{|}{C}-H}}$$

Mechanism:

$$\underset{\text{H H}}{\overset{\text{H Cl}}{H-\overset{|}{\underset{|}{C}}-\overset{|}{\underset{|}{C}}-H}} \xrightarrow{^-\text{OH}} \underset{\text{transition state}}{\left[\begin{array}{c} \text{H} \quad\quad\, ^{\ominus}\text{Cl} \\ H-\overset{|}{C}-----\overset{|}{C}-H \\ \underset{\underset{\text{OH}}{\sigma^-}}{H}\,\,\,\, \text{H} \end{array}\right]} \longrightarrow \underset{\text{H}}{\overset{\text{H}}{H-\overset{|}{C}=\overset{|}{C}-H}}$$

Rate α [alkyl halide × $\overline{\text{OH}}$] → bimolecular → E_2 → concerted reaction.
Differences between E_1 and E_2 are same as SN^1 and SN^2

Note: When aq. KOH is taken for primary alkyl halide nucleophilic substitution reaction takes place.

$$H_2O \quad H_2O \quad H_2O \quad H_2O \quad (\overset{-}{OH}) \quad H_2O \quad H_2O \quad H_2O \quad H_2O$$
aq. KOH

$$ROH \quad (\overset{-}{OH}) \quad ROH \quad ROH$$
alc. KOH

When alcoholic KOH is taken for primary alkyl halides elimination reaction takes place.

(iii) **Elimination Unimolecular via conjugate base (E_1cB):**

$$Cl-\underset{\underset{H}{|}}{\overset{\overset{Cl}{|}}{C}}-\underset{\underset{F}{|}}{\overset{\overset{F}{|}}{C}}-F \xrightarrow{NaOEt} Cl-\underset{}{\overset{\overset{Cl}{|}}{C}}=\underset{}{\overset{\overset{F}{|}}{C}}-F$$

Mechanism:

$$Cl-\underset{\underset{H}{|}}{\overset{\overset{Cl}{|}}{C}}-\underset{\underset{F}{|}}{\overset{\overset{F}{|}}{C}}-F \xrightarrow[fast]{\overset{\ominus}{O}Et} Cl-\underset{\underset{\ominus F}{|}}{\overset{\overset{Cl}{|}}{C}}-\underset{}{\overset{\overset{F}{|}}{C}}-F \xrightarrow{slow} Cl-\overset{\overset{Cl}{|}}{C}=\overset{\overset{F}{|}}{C}-F$$

2.7. Molecular rearrangement reactions

It is further classified into two types.
(1). Intra-molecular rearrangement reactions
(2). Inter-molecular rearrangement reactions.
Most of the molecular rearrangement reactions are intra molecular.

$$H_3C-\overset{H_2}{C}-\overset{H_2}{C}-Br \xrightarrow[\text{1-2, rearrangement}]{AlBr_3} H_3C-\overset{H}{\underset{Br}{C}}-CH_3$$

1-bromopropane   2-bromopropane

Generally 1-2, 2-3, 3-4 rearrangement is possible but not 1-3.

Mechanism:

$$H_3C-\overset{H_2}{C}-\overset{H_2}{C}-Br + AlBr_3 \longrightarrow H_3C-\overset{H}{\underset{H}{C}}-\overset{+}{C}H_2 + \overset{\ominus}{AlBr_4} \longrightarrow H_3C-\overset{H}{\underset{+}{C}}-CH_3 + \overset{\ominus}{AlBr_4} \longrightarrow H_3C-\overset{H}{\underset{Br}{C}}-CH_3$$

1° carbocation less stable   2° carbocation more stable

Carbocation ($\overset{+}{C}$) stability order: 3° – tertiary > 2° – secondary > 1° - primary

2.8. Pericyclic reaction

These are neither radical nor ionic (non radical, non ionic) concerted, reversible reaction proceed via cyclic transition state under thermal or photochemical conditions. It is further classified into three types.

(1). Electrocyclic reaction
(2). Cyclo-addition reaction
(3). Sigmatropic reactions

(1). Electrocyclic reaction

$$\underset{\text{1,3-butadiene}}{\begin{array}{c}HC-CH\\ \parallel \quad \parallel \\ CH_2 \quad CH_2\end{array}} \rightleftharpoons \underset{\text{cyclic transition state}}{\left[\begin{array}{c}HC\text{----}CH\\ \parallel \quad \parallel \\ H_2C\text{----}CH_2\end{array}\right]} \longrightarrow \underset{\text{cyclo-butene}}{\begin{array}{c}HC=CH\\ | \quad | \\ H_2C-CH_2\end{array}}$$

(2). Cyclo-addition reaction.

$$\text{HC}{=}\text{CH}_2 \atop \text{HC}{=}\text{CH}_2 \quad + \quad {\text{CH}_2 \atop \text{CH}_2} \quad \rightleftharpoons \quad \text{cyclic transition state} \quad \rightleftharpoons \quad \text{cyclohexene}$$

1,3-butadiene (diene) + ethylene (dienophile) ⇌ cyclic transition state ⇌ cyclohexene (adduct)

(3). Sigmatropic reaction.

$$R-\underset{\text{(H)}}{\overset{R}{C}}-\overset{H}{C}=CH_2 \quad \rightleftharpoons \quad R_2H_2C \cdots \overset{H\;\;C\;\;H}{\underset{}{\square}} \cdots CH_2 \quad \rightleftharpoons \quad R-\overset{R}{C}=\underset{H}{\overset{}{C}}-CH_2\text{(H)}$$

3. Electronic Displacements in Covalent bond

(1). Inductive effect (IE): permanent effect (polarization effect)
(2). Mesomeric or resonance effect (ME): permanent effect (polarization effect)
(3). Inductomeric effect: temporary effect (polarisability effect)
(4). Electromeric effect: temporary effect (polarisability effect)

3.1. Inductive effect (IE)

Partial polarization of $\bar{e}$ s forming 'σ' bond towards more electronegative atom.

$$H_2\overset{\delta\oplus}{C} \rightarrow \overset{\delta\ominus}{Cl}$$

-ve Inductive effect group (-IE)	+ve Inductive effect group (+IE)
—F, —Cl, —Br, —I, —OH, —OR, —OAr, —NH$_2$, —NR$_2$, —NHR, —O-CO-R, —NH-CHO, —CHO, —CO-R, —COOH, —COOR, —CO-NH$_2$, —CO-Cl, —CO-O-CO-R, Ph, —NO$_2$, —CN, —$\overset{\oplus}{N}H_3$, —$\overset{\oplus}{N}R$, halogens, O, N	—$\overset{\ominus}{O}$, —$\overset{\ominus}{COO}$, —CR$_3$, —CHR$_2$, —CH$_2$R, —CH$_3$, anions and alkyl groups.

| containing groups and cations. | |

Characteristics of inductive effect: It is a permanent effect. It is operated only in sigma (σ) bonds. Only σ electrons are involved. In inductive effect electrons are partially displaced. IE is transmitted along the chain.

$$\overset{\delta\delta\delta\delta\oplus}{C}-\overset{\delta\delta\delta\oplus}{C}-\overset{\delta\delta\oplus}{C}-\overset{\delta\oplus}{C}\rightarrow\overset{\delta\ominus}{Cl}$$

As length of the chain increases the IE decreases.

Applications:
(i) Stability of alkyl carbocations:

$$\overset{\oplus}{C}H_3 \;<\; H_2\overset{\oplus}{C}-CH_3 \;<\; H\overset{\oplus}{C}-CH_3 \;<\; \overset{CH_3}{\underset{CH_3}{\oplus C-CH_3}}$$
$$1° 1° 2° 3°$$
(primary) (primary) (secondary) (tertiary)
less stable ⟶ more stable

+ve Inductive effect (+IE) group will increase the stability of carbocations. As the number of –CH$_3$ increases the stability increases.
For example:

$$H_3C\rightarrow\overset{\oplus}{C}H_2 \quad +IE\ group\ (-CH_3)$$

$$O_2N\leftarrow\overset{\oplus}{C}H_2 \quad -IE\ group\ (-NO_2)$$

$$H_3C\rightarrow\overset{\oplus}{C}H_2 \;>\; O_2N\leftarrow\overset{\oplus}{C}H_2$$

(ii) Acidity of carboxylic compounds:

$$R-\overset{O}{\underset{\|}{C}}-OH \;\underset{}{\overset{-\overset{\oplus}{H}}{\rightleftharpoons}}\; R-\overset{O}{\underset{\|}{C}}-\overset{\ominus}{O}$$

$RCOO^{\ominus}$ Stable than $RCOOH$, ($RCOO^{\ominus} > RCOOH$)

Roll of Inductive effect:

$$H_3C-\underset{\underset{O}{\|}}{C}-OH \xrightleftharpoons{-H^{\oplus}} H_3C-\underset{\underset{O}{\|}}{C}-O^{\ominus}$$

$$Cl-\underset{H_2}{C}-\underset{\underset{O}{\|}}{C}-OH \xrightleftharpoons{-H^{\oplus}} Cl-\underset{H_2}{C}-\underset{\underset{O}{\|}}{C}-O^{\ominus}$$

To know that which is more acidic and stable

$H_3C \rightarrow \underset{\underset{O}{\|}}{C}-O^{\ominus}$ is less stable than $Cl \leftarrow \underset{H_2}{C}-\underset{\underset{O}{\|}}{C}-O^{\ominus}$

+IE →   ← -IE

the '-' effect is more on 'O' hence it is less stable

- effect is stabilised by all the atoms so the '-' charge is less on 'O' so it is stable

$ClCH_2COOH > CH_3COOH$ (acidity order), "−" Inductive effect group (-IE) increases the acidity

e.g.: $ClCH_2COOH < Cl_2CHCOOH < Cl_3CCOOH$

As number of –ve Inductive group increases acidity increases.

e.g.: $Cl\text{-}CH_2COOH < F\text{-}CH_2COOH$

As strength of electro negativity increases the acidity also increases

e.g.:

$Cl-\underset{H_2}{C}-\underset{H_2}{C}-\underset{H_2}{C}-COOH$ (gama) (i)

$H_3C-\underset{\underset{Cl}{|}}{\overset{H}{C}}-\underset{H_2}{C}-COOH$ (beta) (ii)

$H_3C-\underset{H_2}{C}-\underset{\underset{Cl}{|}}{\overset{H}{C}}-COOH$ (alpha) (iii)

Acidity order: (iii) > (ii) > (i). As distance increases the acidity decreases.

Further examples:

(a). HCOOH > H₃C-COOH > H₃C-CH₂-COOH
Among unsubstituted saturated strongest mono-carboxylic acid is formic acid (HCOOH).

(b).
$$\underset{\underset{(-IE)}{\text{oxalic acid}}}{\text{HOOC-COOH}} > \underset{\underset{(+IE)}{\text{acetic acid}}}{\text{H}_3\text{C-COOH}}$$

(c).

$$\underset{\text{oxalic acid}}{\text{HOOC-COOH}} > \underset{\text{malonic acid}}{\text{HOOC-CH}_2\text{-COOH}} > \underset{\text{succinic acid}}{\text{HOOC-CH}_2\text{-CH}_2\text{-COOH}}$$

Among unsubstituted saturated di-carboxylic acids the strongest acid is oxalic acid.

(d). F-COOH < Cl₂CHCOOH

(e).
$$\underset{(-IE)}{\text{HOOC-COOH}} > \underset{(+IE)}{{}^{\ominus}\text{OOC-COOH}}$$

(iii) Basicity of amines:

$$\ddot{\text{N}}\text{H}_3 < \underset{(+IE)}{\text{H}_3\text{C} \rightarrow \ddot{\text{N}}\text{H}_2} < \underset{(2+IE)}{\text{H}_3\text{C} \rightarrow \ddot{\text{N}}\text{H}} \uparrow \text{CH}_3$$

As number of +IE groups increases the basicity increases

$$\underset{(+IE)}{\text{H}_3\text{C} \rightarrow \ddot{\text{N}}\text{H}_2} > \underset{(-IE)}{\text{F}_3\text{C} \leftarrow \ddot{\text{N}}\text{H}_2}$$

3.2. Mesomeric or resonance effect (ME)

It is defined as permanent effect in which π $\bar{e}$ s from a multiple bond completely transfer to an atom (or) single bonds (or) non bonding electrons transfer to an atom to an adjacent single bond. Characteristics of mesomeric effect:

(i). in mesomeric effect the electrons are completely dispersed.

(ii). It is operated in unsaturated compound, especially in conjugated compound.

(iii). In mesomeric effect, π and n - $\bar{e}$ s are involved but not 'σ' $\bar{e}$ s.

'-' Mesomeric groups (-ME)	'+' Mesomeric groups (+ME)
$-\overset{O}{\underset{\|}{C}}-H$, $-\overset{O}{\underset{\|}{C}}-R$,	$-\ddot{\underset{\cdot\cdot}{Cl}}:$, $-\ddot{\underset{\cdot\cdot}{Br}}:$, $-\ddot{\underset{\cdot\cdot}{I}}:$,
$-\overset{O}{\underset{\|}{C}}-OH$, $-\overset{O}{\underset{\|}{C}}-OR$,	$-\ddot{\underset{\cdot\cdot}{O}}H$, $-\ddot{\underset{\cdot\cdot}{O}}R$, $-\ddot{\underset{\cdot\cdot}{S}}H$,
$-\overset{O}{\underset{\|}{C}}-Cl$, $-\overset{O}{\underset{\|}{C}}-NH_2$,	$-\ddot{\underset{\cdot\cdot}{S}}R$, $-\ddot{N}H_2$,
$-\overset{O}{\underset{\|}{C}}-O-\overset{O}{\underset{\|}{C}}-R$, $-\overset{O\diagdown\diagup O}{\underset{\|}{S}}-OH$,	$-\ddot{N}HR$, $-\ddot{N}R_2$,
$-C\equiv N$, $-\overset{\oplus}{\underset{\underset{\ominus}{O}}{N}}=O$	$H \\ -\overset{\|}{\underset{\cdot\cdot}{N}}-\overset{O}{\underset{\|}{C}}-R$,
	$-\ddot{\underset{\cdot\cdot}{O}}-\overset{O}{\underset{\|}{C}}-R$, $-\ddot{\underset{\cdot\cdot}{O}}Ar$,
	$-\ddot{\underset{\cdot\cdot}{O}}Ph$

(iv). It is operated even in the absence of a reagent, i.e. it is a permanent effect.

$$C=C-C=C-C=C-C=O$$

$$H_2C=\underset{H}{\overset{}{C}}-\underset{H}{\overset{}{C}}=O \longleftrightarrow H_2\overset{\ominus}{C}-\underset{H}{\overset{}{C}}=\underset{H}{\overset{}{C}}-\overset{\ominus}{O}$$

'-' mesomeric effect (-ME)

$$H_2C=C-\overset{..}{\underset{..}{Cl}}: \longleftrightarrow H_2\overset{\ominus}{C}-C=\overset{\oplus}{\underset{..}{Cl}}:$$
$$H   H$$

'+' mesomeric effect (+ME)

In –ME group there will be no lone pair electrons.

e.g.

$$-\overset{..}{\underset{..}{O}}-\overset{\overset{O}{\|}}{C}-CH_3 \quad \text{+ME group}$$

$$-\overset{\overset{O}{\|}}{C}-\overset{..}{N}H_2 \quad \text{-ME group}$$

$$-\overset{\overset{:\overset{..}{Cl}:}{|}}{\underset{\underset{:\overset{..}{Cl}:}{|}}{C}}-\overset{..}{\underset{..}{Cl}}: \quad \text{not either +ME or -ve}$$

$$-\overset{\overset{H}{|}}{\underset{\underset{H}{|}}{C}}-H \quad \text{not either +ME or -ve}$$

Applications:

(1). Stability of allyl and benzyl carbocations:

Allyl carbocations:

$$H_2C=C-\overset{\oplus}{C}H_2 \longleftrightarrow H_2\overset{\oplus}{C}-C=CH_2 \quad$$ allyl carbocation is the carbocation
$$H   H $$ which is next to double bond

1° carbocation

$$H_2C=\overset{b}{C}-\overset{H}{\underset{\oplus}{C}}-\overset{a}{C}=CH_2 \overset{a}{\longleftrightarrow} H_2C=C-C=C-\overset{\oplus}{C}H_2$$
$$H H   HHH$$

$\updownarrow b$ \quad 2° carbocation

$$\overset{\oplus}{H_2C}-C=C-C=CH_2$$
$$HHH$$

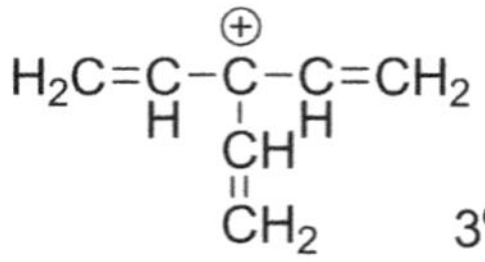

$$H_2C=C-\overset{+}{\underset{|}{C}}-C=CH_2$$
$$H\underset{||}{CH}H$$
$$CH_2 \quad \text{3° carbocation}$$

Order of stability of allyl carbocations: 3° > 2° > 1°

Benzyl carbocations:

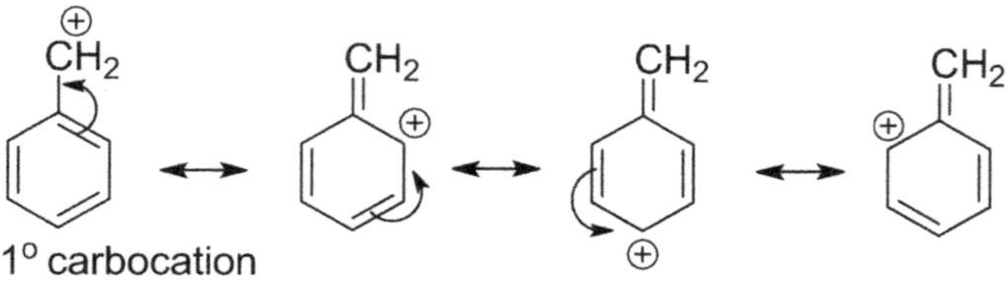

$\overset{+}{CH_2}$ ↔ CH_2 ↔ CH_2 ↔ CH_2

1° carbocation

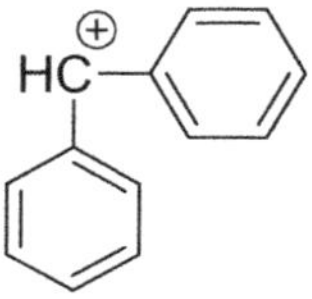

2° carbocation 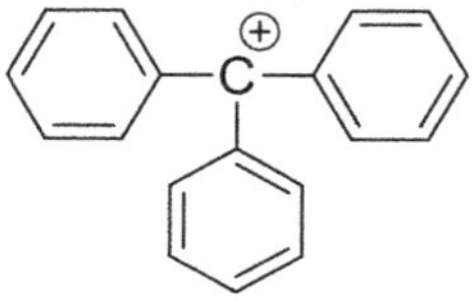   3° carbocation

Stability of benzyl carbocations: 3° > 2° > 1°

e.g. Allyl carbocation is more stable than alkyl carbocation.

$$H_2C=\underset{H}{C}-\overset{+}{CH_2} \quad > \quad H_3C-\overset{+}{\underset{\underset{CH_3}{|}}{C}}-CH_3$$

allyl (1°) alkyl (3°)

(2). Stability of allyl and benzyl free radicals:

Allyl free radicals:

$$H_2C=\underset{H}{C}-\overset{\bullet}{C}H_2 \quad \longleftrightarrow \quad H_2\overset{\bullet}{C}-\underset{H}{C}=CH_2$$

1° free radical

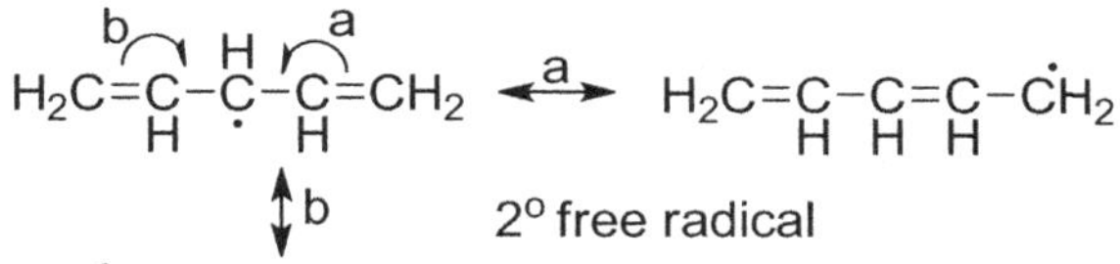

$$H_2C=C-C-C=CH_2 \underset{}{\overset{a}{\longleftrightarrow}} H_2\overset{\cdot}{C}=C-C=C-\overset{\cdot}{C}H_2$$

(positions labeled b, H, a on left structure; H, H below)

2° free radical

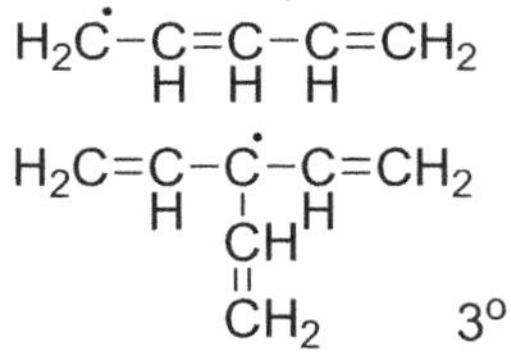

$$\updownarrow b$$

$$H_2\overset{\cdot}{C}-C=C-C=CH_2$$

$$H_2C=C-\overset{\cdot}{C}-C=CH_2$$
$$\quad\quad\ \ |\ \ $$
$$\quad\quad CH$$
$$\quad\quad\ \|$$
$$\quad\quad CH_2 \quad\quad 3° \text{ free radical}$$

Stability order of allyl free radicals: 3° > 2° > 1°

Benzyl free radicals:

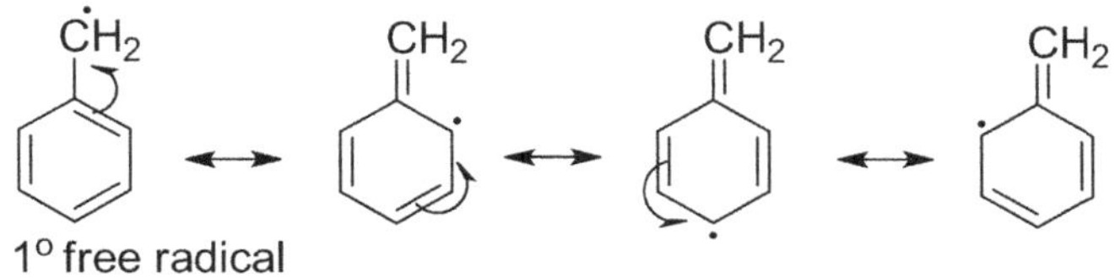

(resonance structures of benzyl radical shown)

1° free radical

(diphenylmethyl and triphenylmethyl radical structures)

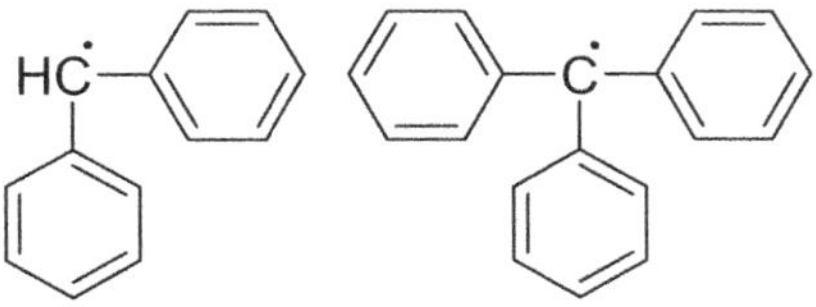

2° free radical   3° free radical

Stability of benzyl free radicals: 3° > 2° > 1°

(3). Acidity of carboxylic acids and phenols:

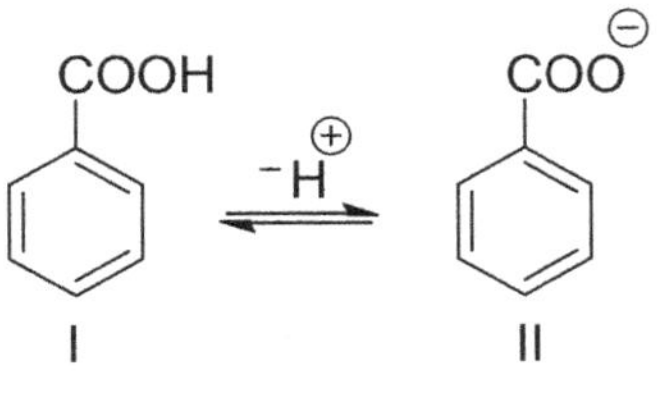

(benzoic acid $\rightleftharpoons$ benzoate anion, $-H^+$)

I   II

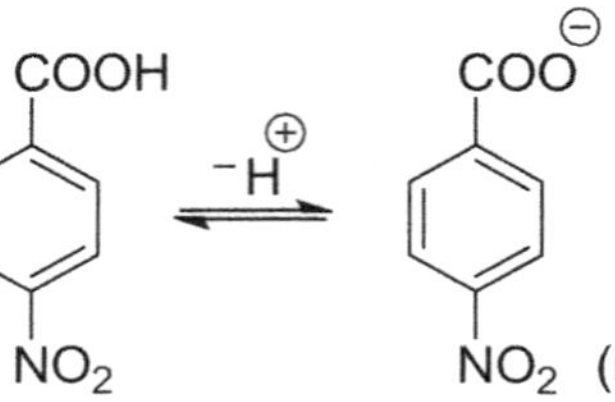

$$\underset{\text{III}}{\text{C}_6\text{H}_4(\text{COOH})(\text{NO}_2)} \underset{-H^+}{\rightleftharpoons} \underset{\text{IV}}{\text{C}_6\text{H}_4(\text{COO}^-)(\text{NO}_2)} \quad (\text{NO}_2 \text{ is -ME group})$$

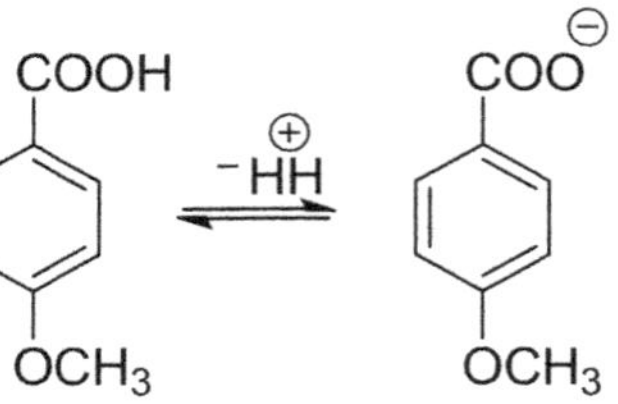

$$\underset{\text{V}}{\text{C}_6\text{H}_4(\text{COOH})(\text{OCH}_3)} \underset{-H^+}{\rightleftharpoons} \underset{\text{VI}}{\text{C}_6\text{H}_4(\text{COO}^-)(\text{OCH}_3)} \quad (\text{OCH}_3 \text{ is +ME group})$$

Stability of conjugate bases: IV > II > VI
Order of acidity: III > I > V
"-" Mesomeric effect (-ME) group increases acidity.
e.g.

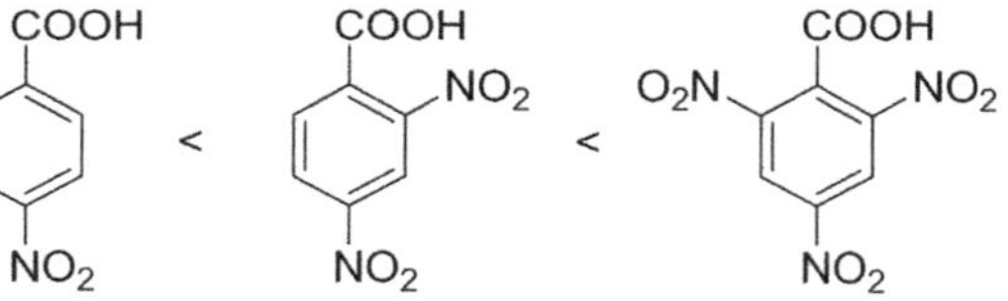

$$\underset{\text{I}}{\text{4-NO}_2\text{-C}_6\text{H}_4\text{-COOH}} < \underset{\text{II}}{\text{3,4-(NO}_2)_2\text{-C}_6\text{H}_3\text{-COOH}} < \underset{\text{III}}{\text{3,4,5-(NO}_2)_3\text{-C}_6\text{H}_2\text{-COOH}}$$

acidity order: III > II > I

Basicity of amines:

I: *p*-methoxyaniline with $\ddot{N}H_2$ and OCH_3 groups (OCH$_3$ is +ME group)

II: aniline with $\ddot{N}H_2$ group

III: *p*-nitroaniline with $\ddot{N}H_2$ and NO_2 groups (NO$_2$ is −ME group)

basicity order: I > II > III

3.3. Inductomeric effect

Increase in inductive effect in the presence of a reagent is known as Inductomeric effect. It is a temporary effect.

$$\overset{\delta\oplus\delta\ominus}{R \leftarrow Cl}$$ It is closely related to inductive effect.

3.4. Electromeric effect

Mesomeric effect which is operated only in the presence of a reagent is known as electromeric effect.
e.g.

$$\underset{}{\overset{}{C=C}} + \underset{reagent}{HBr} \longrightarrow C_2H_5Br$$

These Inductomeric effect and electromeric effects are temporary effects only.

3.5. Hyperconjugation

Hyperconjugation: The delocalization of alpha (α) carbon sigma (σ) bond electrons is known as hyperconjugation.

$$\begin{array}{c}\text{alpha} \rightarrow H \leftarrow \text{sigma bond} \\ \text{hydrogen} \; C-C=C \\ \nearrow \quad C=O \\ \text{alpha} \quad C=N \\ \text{carbon} \quad C\equiv C \\ C\equiv N \end{array}$$

e.g.

$$H-\underset{H}{\overset{H}{C}}-\underset{H}{\overset{H}{C}}=O \leftrightarrow H-C=\underset{H}{\overset{H^{\oplus}\;H}{C}}-O^{\ominus} \leftrightarrow H-\underset{H^{\oplus}}{\overset{H\;\;H}{C}}=C-O^{\ominus} \leftrightarrow \overset{\oplus}{H}\;\underset{H}{\overset{H\;H}{C}}=C-O^{\ominus}$$

(hyperconjugated substance)

$$\underset{\text{alpha}}{\overset{H}{C}}-\overset{\oplus}{C} \quad (\text{or}) \quad \underset{\text{alpha}}{\overset{H}{C}}-\overset{\cdot}{C}$$

At least one unsaturated carbocation or free radical with alpha (α) - carbon then only hyperconjugation will take place.

(a). Stability of alkenes: By hyperconjugation method

$$H_2C=CH_2 \quad H_3C-\underset{H}{C}=CH_2 \quad H_3C-\underset{H\;H}{C}=C-CH_3 \quad H_3C-\underset{H}{\overset{CH_3}{C}}=C-CH_3 \quad H_3C-\overset{CH_3}{C}=\underset{CH_3}{C}-CH_3$$

(I)   (II)   (III)   (IV)   (V)

(I) No α – carbons, no hyperconjugation
(II) 3α – (CH_3), 3 hyperconjugation structures
(III) 6α – (CH_3), 6 hyperconjugation structures
(IV) 9α – (CH_3), 9 hyperconjugation structures
(V) 12α – (CH_3), 12 hyperconjugation structures
Stability order: V > IV > III > II > I
e.g.: (II) 3α – (CH_3), 3 hyperconjugation structures

$$\underset{\overset{|}{\overset{\oplus}{H}}}{\overset{H}{\underset{|}{H-C}}}=\underset{H}{\overset{|}{C}}-\overset{\ominus}{\underset{}{C}H_2} \longleftrightarrow \underset{\overset{|}{H}}{\overset{H}{\underset{|}{H-C}}}\overset{\curvearrowright}{\underset{}{C}}=CH_2 \longleftrightarrow \underset{\overset{|}{H}}{\overset{\overset{\oplus}{H}}{\underset{|}{H-C}}}=\underset{H}{\overset{|}{C}}-\overset{\ominus}{C}H_2$$

(II)

$$\overset{\oplus}{H} \underset{\overset{|}{H}}{\overset{H}{\underset{|}{C}}}=C-\overset{\ominus}{C}H_2$$

3 - hyperconjugation structures

Stability of alkenes is measured by only by hyperconjugation.

As number of α – carbons are increases the stability of alkenes increases.

(b). Stability of alkyl carbocations:

$$\underset{\overset{\oplus}{H}}{\overset{H}{\underset{|}{H-C}}}=CH_2 \longleftrightarrow \underset{\overset{|}{H}}{\overset{H}{\underset{|}{H-C}}}\overset{\oplus}{\underset{}{C}}H_2 \longleftrightarrow \underset{\overset{|}{H}}{\overset{\overset{\oplus}{H}}{\underset{|}{H-C}}}=CH_2$$

(II)

$$\overset{\oplus}{H} \underset{\overset{|}{H}}{\overset{H}{\underset{|}{C}}}=CH_2$$ 3 α Hydrogens
3 hyperconjugations

e.g.: (II) 3α – Hydrogens, 3 hyperconjugation structures

$$\underset{\overset{\oplus}{H}}{\overset{H}{\underset{|}{H-C}}}=CH_2 \longleftrightarrow \underset{\overset{|}{H}}{\overset{H}{\underset{|}{H-C}}}\overset{\oplus}{\underset{}{C}}H_2 \longleftrightarrow \underset{\overset{|}{H}}{\overset{\overset{\oplus}{H}}{\underset{|}{H-C}}}=CH_2$$

(II)

$$\overset{\oplus}{H} \underset{\overset{|}{H}}{\overset{H}{\underset{|}{C}}}=CH_2$$ 3 α Hydrogens
3 hyperconjugations

e.g.:

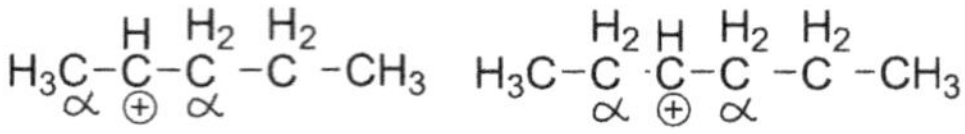

$$H_3C-\underset{\underset{\alpha}{\bullet}}{\overset{H}{C}}-\underset{\oplus}{\overset{H_2}{C}}-\overset{H_2}{\underset{\alpha}{C}}-CH_3 \qquad H_3C-\overset{H_2}{\underset{\alpha}{C}}-\underset{\oplus}{\overset{H}{\underset{\bullet}{C}}}-\overset{H_2}{\underset{\alpha}{C}}-\overset{H_2}{C}-CH_3$$

(I) 3 + 2 = 5α , (I) 2 + 2 = 4α

Stability: I > II

(c). Stability of alkyl free radicals:

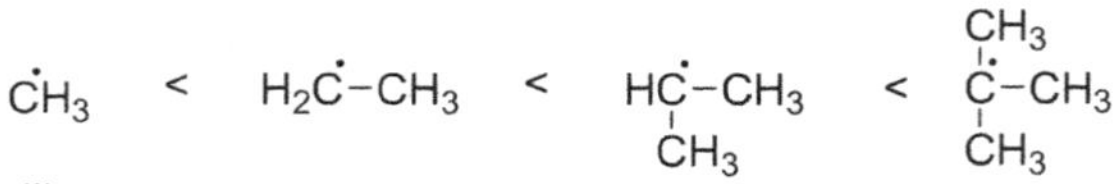

$$\overset{\bullet}{C}H_3 \;<\; H_2\overset{\bullet}{C}-CH_3 \;<\; \underset{CH_3}{\overset{\bullet}{H}\overset{|}{C}-CH_3} \;<\; \underset{CH_3}{\overset{CH_3}{\overset{|}{\overset{\bullet}{C}}-CH_3}}$$

(I) (II) (III) (IV)
no alpha 3 alpha 6 alpha 9 alpha
no hc 3 hc 6 hc 9 hc

e.g.:

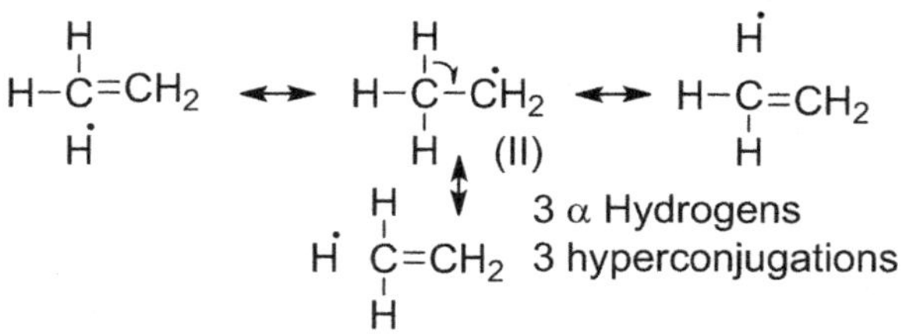

$$H-\underset{\overset{\bullet}{H}}{\overset{H}{C}}=CH_2 \;\longleftrightarrow\; H-\underset{H}{\overset{H}{\overset{|}{C}}}\overset{\bullet}{-}CH_2 \;\longleftrightarrow\; H-\underset{H}{\overset{\overset{\bullet}{H}}{C}}=CH_2$$

(II)

3 α Hydrogens
3 hyperconjugations

(d). Orienting influence of alkyl groups:

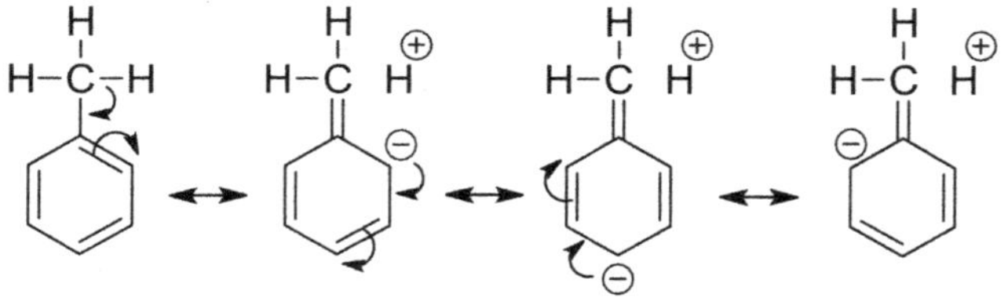

[resonance structures of toluene/methylbenzene cation showing hyperconjugation]

Further examples:

If H_3C-C saturated $<$ $H_3C-\underset{CH_3}{\overset{CH_3}{\overset{|}{C}}-C}$ saturated } by means of Inductive Effect

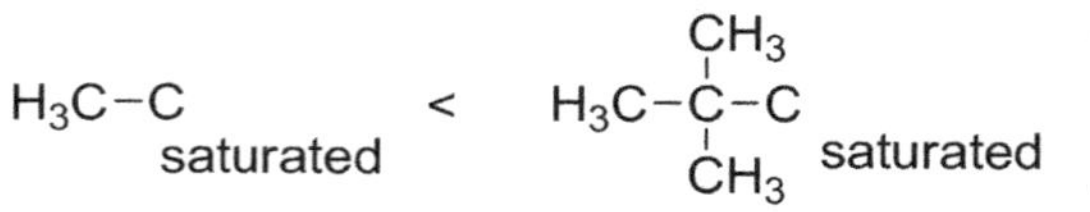

But   H₃C−C=   >   H₃C−C(CH₃)(CH₃)−C=   } by means of
          unsaturated   unsaturated   } hyperconjugation

\# Mesomeric effect (more powerful) > Hyperconjugation > Inductive Effect.

4. Acidity and Basicity of Organic Molecules

$$H-A + H_2O \rightleftharpoons H_3O^+ + A^-$$
acid — base — conjugate acid — conjugate base

$$K_{eq} = \frac{[H_3O^+][A^-]}{[H-A][H_2O]}$$

$$K_{eq} = [H_2O] = K_a = \frac{[H_3O^+][A^-]}{[H-A]}$$

$K_a \, \alpha$ acidity

$K_a \, \alpha$ acidity: Experimentally measure K_a value of organic molecules is very less so we can show the K_a value in terms of PK_a value

$$PK_a \propto \frac{1}{K_a}$$

$$PK_a \propto \frac{1}{acidity}$$

4.1 Acidity of carboxylic acids:

$$R-\overset{O}{\underset{}{C}}-\overset{\ominus}{OH} \leftrightarrow R-\overset{\overset{\ominus}{O}}{\underset{}{C}}=\overset{\oplus}{O}-H \rightleftharpoons R-\overset{O}{\underset{}{C}}-\overset{\ominus}{O} \leftrightarrow R-\overset{\ominus}{\underset{}{C}}=O$$

According to resonance rules the resonance with single charge are more stable than the resonance structure with charge separation ($\overset{\ominus}{O} > \overset{\oplus}{O}$).

According to resonance equivalent which are more stable than non-equal resonance

$$\underset{(I)}{R-\overset{O}{\underset{\|}{C}}-\overset{\ominus}{O}} \quad > \quad \underset{(II)}{R-\overset{O}{\underset{\|}{C}}-OH}$$

Acid structure (I) is more resonance stabilized than acid structure (II).

For example, between

$$\underset{\text{less acidic}}{Cl_3CCOOH} < \underset{\text{more acidic}}{F_3CCOOH}$$

Acidity is more of F_3C-COOH than PK_a is less (because $PK_a \propto$ 1/acidity).

Effect of chelation:

$$\underset{\text{maleic acid}}{\begin{matrix} H-C-\overset{O}{\underset{\|}{C}}-OH \\ H-C-\underset{\|}{C}-OH \\ O \end{matrix}} \xrightarrow{-\overset{\oplus}{H}} \underset{\text{maleate ion}}{\begin{matrix} H-C-\overset{O}{\underset{\|}{C}}-\overset{\ominus}{O} \\ H-C-\underset{\|}{C}-O-H \\ O \end{matrix}} \leftarrow \text{chelation}$$

[Fumaric acid ⇌ Fumarate ion equilibrium shown]

fumaric acid → fumarate ion (−H⁺)

Stability: maleate ion > fumarate ion
Acidity: maleic acid > fumaric acid
For example: (I) salicylic acid (II) p-hydroxy benzoic acid (III) 2,6-dihydroxy benzoic acid

(I) salicylic acid ⇌ salicylate ion (−H⁺) — chelate intramolecular hydrogen bonding

(II) p-hydroxy benzoic acid ⇌ p-hydroxy benzoic ion (−H⁺)

(III) 2,6-dihydroxy benzoic acid ⇌ 2,6-dihydroxy benzoic ion (−H⁺)

Stability: (III) 2,6-dihydroxy benzoic acid > (I) salicylate ion > (II) p-hydroxy benzoic ion

Acidity: (III) 2,6-dihydroxy benzoic acid > (I) salicylate ion > (II) p-hydroxy benzoic ion

Effect of position:

(I) 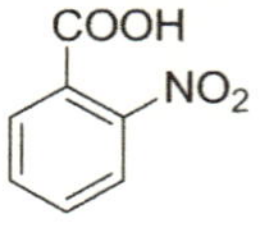
ortho-nitro benzoic acid (COOH, NO₂ ortho)
meta-nitro benzoic acid 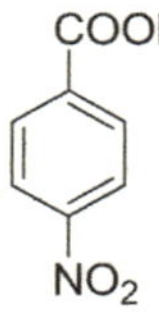
para-nitro benzoic acid

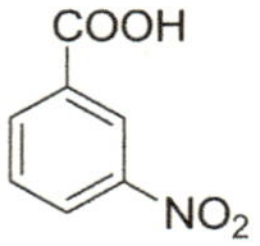

(II) 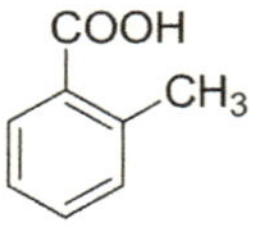
ortho-methyl benzoic acid 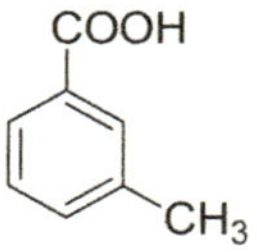
meta-methyl benzoic acid 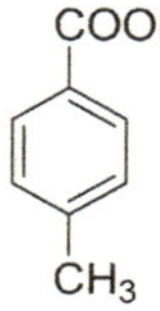
para-methyl benzoic acid

In general irrespective of nature of substitute, *ortho*-substituted benzoic acids are more acidic than isomeric *meta* and *para* benzoic acid. This is due to *ortho*-effect which can be explained by steric-crowdiness.

The Substituent which is present at ortho (or) para position can show it's electronic effect more effectively than the substituent which is present at meta position.

(I) electron withdrawing group (NO_2): order of acidity: ortho > meta > para

(II) electron donating group (CH_3): order of acidity: ortho > meta > para

ortho is more acidic than meta and para

e.g:-

(I)

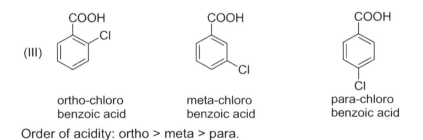

pthalic acid   isopthalic acid   terepthalic acid

Order of acidity: pthalic acid > isopthalic acid > terephthalic acid

(II)

salicilic acid   meta-salicilic acid   para-salicilic acid

Order of acidity: salicilic acid > meta-salicilic acid > para-salicilic acid

(III)

ortho-chloro benzoic acid   meta-chloro benzoic acid   para-chloro benzoic acid

Order of acidity: ortho > meta > para.

4.2. Acidity of Phenols

Phenol (I) is more resonance stabilized than Phenol (II).

Order of acidity: V > IV > III > II > I.

Effect of position of acidity of phenols:-

ortho > para > meta

Order of acidity: ortho > para > meta.

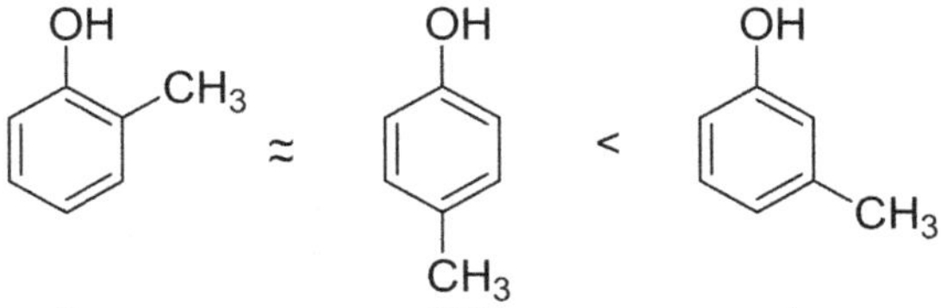

OH
    CH₃   OH   OH
ortho ≈   para   <   meta
             CH₃   CH₃

Order of acidity: meta > ortho ≈ para.

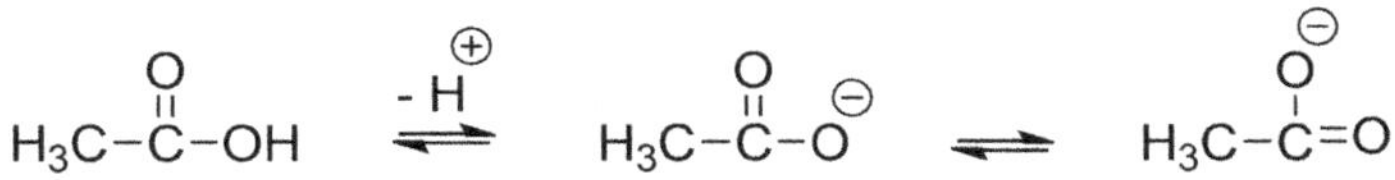

$$H_3C-\overset{O}{\underset{}{C}}-OH \xrightleftharpoons{-H^+} H_3C-\overset{O}{\underset{}{C}}-O^- \rightleftharpoons H_3C-\overset{O^-}{\underset{}{C}}=O$$

Acetic acid is having the equivalent resonance structures.

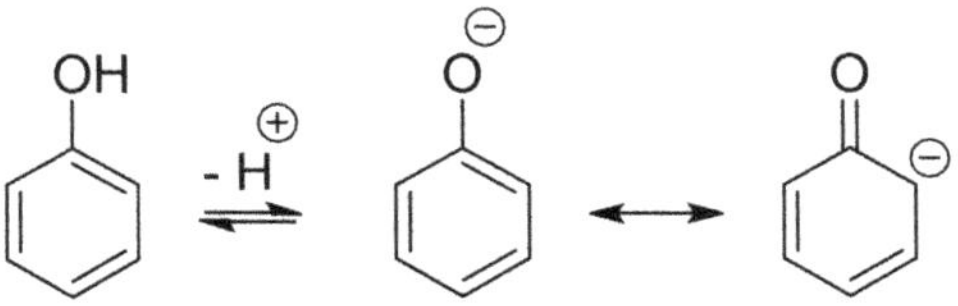

Phenol $\xrightleftharpoons{-H^+}$ phenoxide (stable) ↔ cyclohexadienone anion (less stable)

Negative charge $\ominus$ on Carbon is less stable than Oxygen so $CH_3COO^{\ominus}$ is more acidic than $C_6H_5O^{\ominus}$

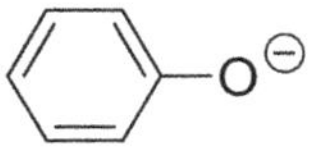

Ka value of caboxilic acids ~ 10^{-4}
Ka value of Phenol ~ 10^{-10}

Generally phenols are insoluble in NaHCO₃ (bicarbonates). But, the picric acid is soluble.

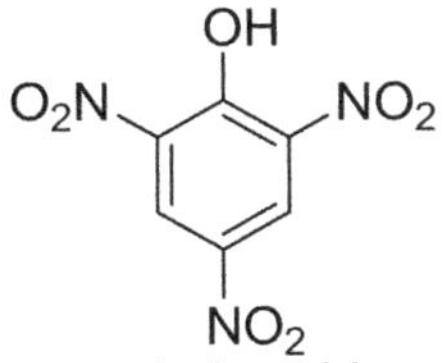

picric acid: 2,4,6-trinitrophenol (OH with O₂N groups at 2, 4, 6 positions)

Because it forms salts with NaHCO₃ and liberates CO₂ very easily.

4.3. Acidity of Alcohols

$$RO-H \xrightarrow{-H^+} RO^-$$

Alcohols are acidic in nature because H⁺ is attached to highly electro negative 'Oxygen' which withdraw the electron density from 'Carbon' and releases H⁺

$$H_2O \xrightleftharpoons{-H^+} {}^-OH$$

Water (H_2O) is more acidic than alcohols (ROH).
Ka value of $H_2O \rightarrow 10^{-14}$
Ka value of ROH $\rightarrow 10^{-16}$ to 10^{-18}
For example:

$$RCH_2OH \xrightarrow{-H^+} RCH_2O^- \quad 1° \text{ (primary)}$$

$$R_2CHOH \xrightarrow{-H^+} R_2CHO^- \quad 2° \text{ (secondary)}$$

$$R_3COH \xrightarrow{-H^+} R_3CO^- \quad 3° \text{ (tertiary)}$$

Stability of alcoxides : 1° > 2° > 3°
Acidity of alcoxides : 1° > 2° > 3°

CH_3OH > CH_3CH_2OH
more acidic

4.4 Acidity of 1-alkynes

$$R-C\equiv C-H \xrightarrow{-H^+} R-C\equiv C^-$$

sp ↗ acidic H

Acidity depends on Hybridization, so

$$Csp > Csp^2 > Csp^3$$

As 'S' character increases the acidity increases.
For example:

$$\equiv C-H \quad > \quad =C-H \quad > \quad -C-H$$
$$(sp) \qquad (sp^2) \qquad (sp^3)$$

Ka value for $R-C\equiv C-H$ is $\rightarrow 10^{-25}$

These are less acidic than alcohols and H_2O.

Alkenes = Ka values are 10^{-35}

Alkanes = Ka values are 10^{-45}

Ka values of alkenes and alkanes are very small (i.e. 10^{-35} and 10^{-45}) so, these are not acidic.

Complete order of acidity:

Carboxilic acids > Phenols > H_2O > ROH > $R-C\equiv C-H$

$$RCOO^\ominus > ArO^\ominus > {}^\ominus OH > RO^\ominus > R-C\equiv C^\ominus$$

4.5. BASICITY

K_b = basicity
[PK_b = 1/basicity]
Lewis bases = which donates e- pair.

4.6. Aliphatic Amines:

$$H_3C-\overset{..}{N}H_2 \qquad H_3C-\overset{H}{\underset{..}{N}}-CH_3 \qquad H_3C-\overset{..}{\underset{CH_3}{N}}-CH_3$$

1° (primary) 2° (secondary) 3° (tertiary)

Availability of electron density, basicity is more steric hindrance would be less on e- pair donating atom. So if steric hindrance is more basicity will be less.

Therefore highly electron density and less steric hindrance will be highly basic.

Basicity of amines: 2° > 1° > 3°

$$\overset{\diagdown}{\underset{\diagup}{C}}-\overset{..}{\underset{\underset{|}{C}}{N}}-\overset{\diagup}{\underset{\diagdown}{C}}-$$ 3° (tertiary)
highly steric hindrance, hence it will not donate e- pair easily

2° > 1° more basic because of e- density.
1° > 3° more basic because of more steric hindrance.

4.7. Aromatic Amines

$H_3C-\ddot{N}H_2$

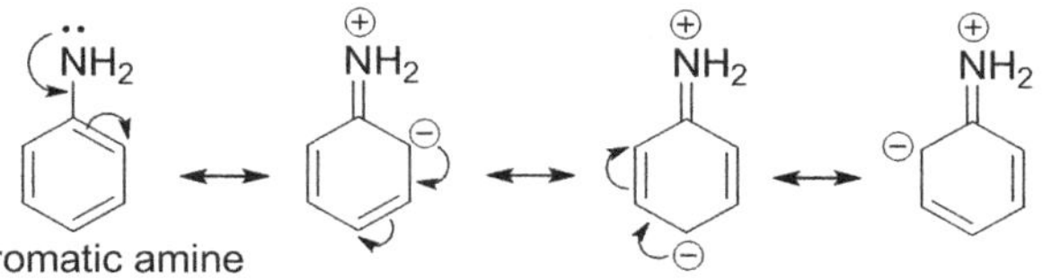

aliphatic amine   aromatic amine

Aromatic amines e- density is lesser than aliphatic amines.
Aromatic amines highly steric hindrance than aliphatic amines.
So aliphatic amines are more basic than aromatic amines.
Basicity of amines: Aliphatic amines > Aromatic amines
Kb of aromatic amines $\rightarrow 10^{-10}$
Kb of aliphatic amine $\rightarrow 10^{-4}$

Effect of position (substituent):

(I)

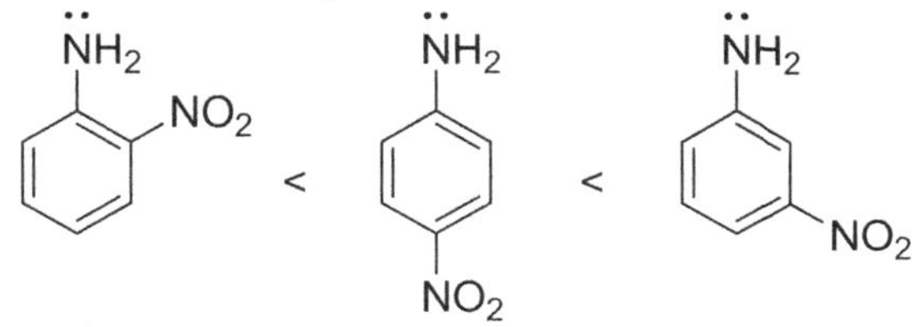

ortho < para < meta

(II)

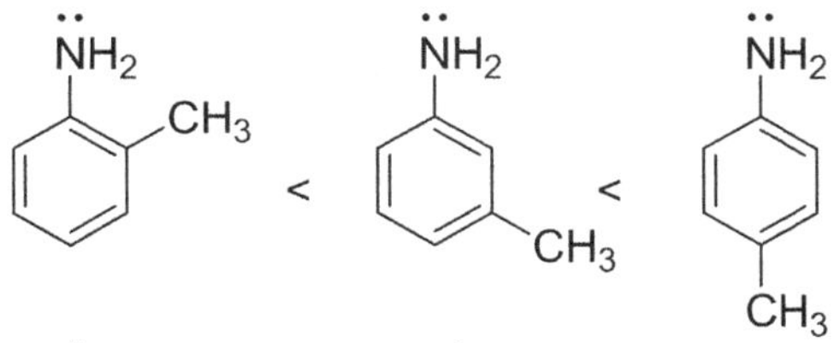

ortho < meta < para

Order of basicity: In general irrespective nature of the substituent ortho substituted amines are less basic than isomeric 'meta' and 'para' substituted benzenes.

I = ortho < para < meta
II = ortho < meta < para

This is due to ortho effect which can be explained by steric hindrance.

When e- withdrawing group (-NO$_2$) is present density decreases and basicity decreases.

When e- donating group (-CH$_3$) is present density increases and basicity increases.

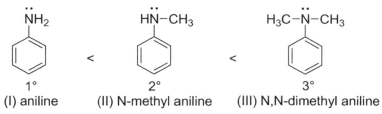

ortho-phenylene diamine   meta-phenylene diamine   para-phenylene diamine

1°, 2°, 3° Aromatic amines:

$$\underset{\underset{\text{(I) aniline}}{1°}}{\overset{\overset{..}{NH_2}}{\bigcirc}} \quad < \quad \underset{\underset{\text{(II) N-methyl aniline}}{2°}}{\overset{\overset{..}{HN-CH_3}}{\bigcirc}} \quad < \quad \underset{\underset{\text{(III) N,N-dimethyl aniline}}{3°}}{\overset{\overset{..}{H_3C-N-CH_3}}{\bigcirc}}$$

From (I) to (III) electron density increases.
From (I) to (III) steric hindrance increases.
Mainly based on availability of e- density.
For example: in below example steric effect is very high.

Ph-NH₂ (1°) > Ph₂NH (2°) > Ph₃N (3°)

4.8. Basicity of Amides

(a) $R-\underset{\underset{NH_2}{\|}}{\overset{O}{C}} \longleftrightarrow R-\underset{\underset{NH_2}{\|}}{\overset{O^-}{C}}{}^{+}$ because < $R-NH_2$ (amines)

(b) $R-\underset{\|}{\overset{O}{C}}-NH_2$ < $H_2N-\underset{\|}{\overset{O}{C}}-NH_2$
   basicity

(c) aniline ($Ph-NH_2$) > acetanilide ($Ph-NH-\underset{\|}{\overset{O}{C}}-CH_3$, amide)
   basicity

Amides basicity is very less so these are considered as neutral.
Basicity order: cyanides < imines < amines.

$$R-C\equiv\overset{..}{N} \quad < \quad R-\underset{H}{\overset{..}{C}}=\overset{..}{N}H \quad < \quad R-\overset{H_2}{C}-\overset{..}{N}H_2$$

(sp)   (sp^2)   (sp^3)
cyanides   imines   amines

Electro-negativity: $N_{Sp} > N_{Sp2} > N_{Sp3}$
Cyanides are very very less basic.

5. Isomerism and Stereochemistry Basics

Isomerism:
Compounds having same molecular formula are known as isomers. But, these isomers exhibit different physical and chemical properties.

5.1. Classification of Isomers

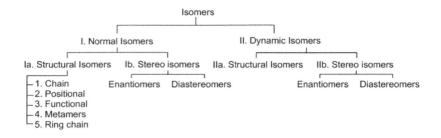

1. Normal Isomers: Which not convertible at lower temperature.
e.g.: CH_3CH_2OH and CH_3OCH_3.

Ia. Structural Isomers: Same molecular formula, but differ in structure, e.g.: CH_3CH_2OH and CH_3OCH_3.

1. Chain isomers: (4-Carbons are needed) same molecular formula but having different chain structure.
e.g.: n-butane and iso-butane

$$H_3C-\underset{}{\overset{H_2}{C}}-\underset{}{\overset{H_2}{C}}-CH_3 \quad \longleftarrow \quad C_4H_{10} \quad \longrightarrow \quad H_3C-\underset{H}{\overset{CH_3}{C}}-CH_3$$

n-butate iso-butane

2. Positional isomers: Same molecular formula and same chain but different position of atoms or groups.
e.g.: 1-chloro-butane and 2-chloro-butane

$$H_3C-\overset{H_2}{C}-\overset{H_2}{C}-\underset{Cl}{CH_2} \quad \longleftarrow \quad C_4H_9Cl \quad \longrightarrow \quad H_3C-\overset{H_2}{C}-\underset{Cl}{\overset{H}{C}}-CH_3$$

1-chloro-butane 2-chloro-butane

n-propanol and iso-propanol

$$H_3C-\overset{H_2}{C}-\overset{H_2}{C}-OH \quad \longleftarrow \quad C_3H_8O \quad \longrightarrow \quad H_3C-\underset{H}{\overset{OH}{C}}-CH_3$$

n-propanol iso-propanol

For example:

$$\underset{\underset{CH_3}{|}}{\overset{\overset{CH_3}{|}}{H_3C-C}}-\overset{H_2}{C}-Cl \longleftarrow C_5H_{11}Cl \longrightarrow \underset{\underset{Cl}{|}}{\overset{\overset{CH_3}{|}}{H_3C-C}}-\overset{H_2}{C}-CH_3$$

chain isomerism

If chain is same and molecular formula same and position is different then only positional isomerism.

3. Functional groups: Same molecular formula but different functional groups.

(a) Alkynes and Alkadienes:

$$\underset{\text{alkyne}}{H_3C-C\equiv C-H} \longleftarrow \underset{C_nH_{2n-2}}{C_3H_4} \longrightarrow \underset{\text{alkadiene}}{H_2C=C=CH_2}$$

(b) Alcohols and Ethers:

$$\underset{\text{alcohol}}{H_3C-\overset{H_2}{C}-OH} \longleftarrow \underset{C_nH_{2n+2}O}{C_2H_6O} \longrightarrow \underset{\text{ether}}{H_3C-O-CH_3}$$

(c) Aldehydes and Ketones:

$$\underset{\text{aldehyde}}{H_3C-\overset{H_2}{C}-\overset{\overset{O}{\|}}{C}-H} \longleftarrow \underset{C_nH_{2n}O}{C_3H_6O} \longrightarrow \underset{\text{ketone}}{H_3C-\overset{\overset{O}{\|}}{C}-CH_3}$$

Unsaturated alcohols and unsaturated ether

$$\underset{\text{unsaturated alcohol}}{H_2C=\underset{H}{\overset{}{C}}-\overset{H_2}{C}-OH} \longleftarrow \underset{C_nH_{2n}O}{C_3H_6O} \longrightarrow \underset{\text{unsaturated ether}}{H_2C=\underset{H}{\overset{}{C}}-O-CH_3}$$

(d) Carboxylic acids, esters, hydroxyl carbonyl compounds and alkoxy-carbonyl compounds.

$$\underset{C_nH_{2n}O_2}{C_2H_4O_2} \longrightarrow \underset{\text{carboxylic acid}}{H_3C-\overset{\overset{O}{\|}}{C}-OH} \quad \underset{\text{ester}}{H-\overset{\overset{O}{\|}}{C}-OCH_3} \quad \underset{\text{hydroxy aldehyde}}{HO-\overset{H_2}{C}-\overset{\overset{O}{\|}}{C}-H}$$

(e) Nitro alkanes and Alkyl nitrites:

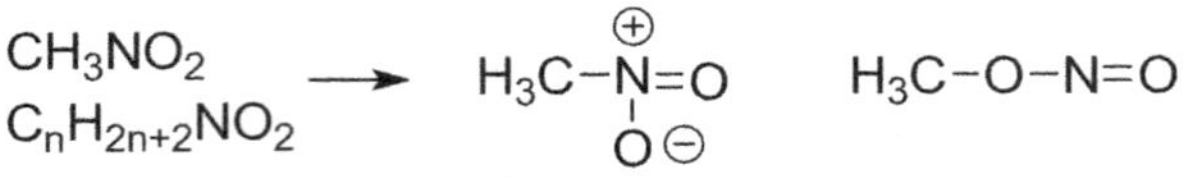

CH_3NO_2
$C_nH_{2n+2}NO_2$ ⟶ $H_3C-\overset{\oplus}{\underset{\underset{O^{\ominus}}{|}}{N}}=O$ $H_3C-O-N=O$

nitro-alkane   alkyl-nitrite

(f) 1°, 2°, 3°- Amines:

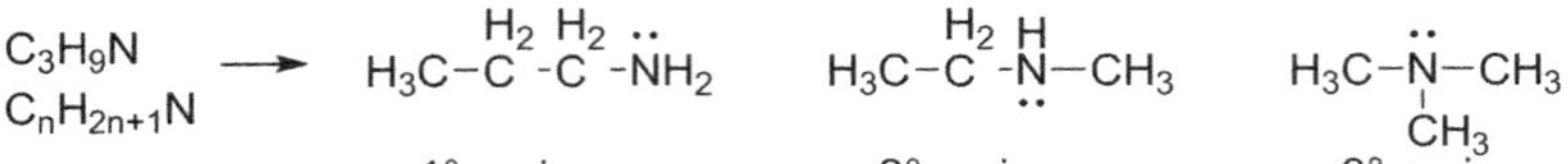

C_3H_9N
$C_nH_{2n+1}N$ ⟶ $H_3C-\overset{H_2}{C}-\overset{H_2}{\underset{}{C}}-\overset{..}{N}H_2$ $H_3C-\overset{H_2}{C}-\overset{H}{\underset{..}{N}}-CH_3$ $H_3C-\overset{..}{\underset{\underset{CH_3}{|}}{N}}-CH_3$

   1°-amine   2°-amine   3°-amine

(g) Cyanides and isocyanides:

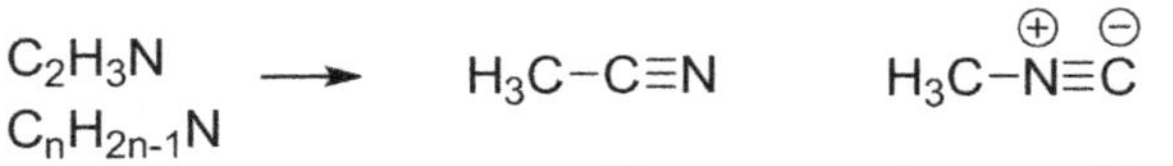

C_2H_3N
$C_nH_{2n-1}N$ ⟶ $H_3C-C\equiv N$ $H_3C-\overset{\oplus}{N}\equiv\overset{\ominus}{C}$

cyanide   iso-cyanide

(i) Benzoic acid is isomeric with phenyl formate

$Ph-\overset{O}{\underset{}{\overset{||}{C}}}-O-H$ $H-\overset{O}{\underset{}{\overset{||}{C}}}-O-Ph$

benzoic acid   phenyl formate

4. Metamers: Differ in sizes of two alkyl groups attached to functional group with same molecular formula.

e.g.:

a) $C_2H_5-O-C_2H_5$ and $H_3C-O-C_3H_7$

b) 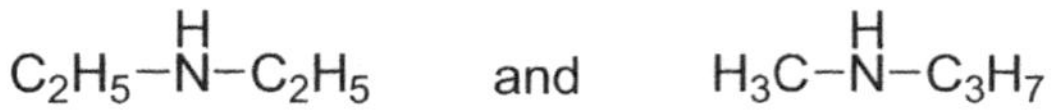 $C_2H_5-\overset{H}{\underset{}{N}}-C_2H_5$ and $H_3C-\overset{H}{\underset{}{N}}-C_3H_7$

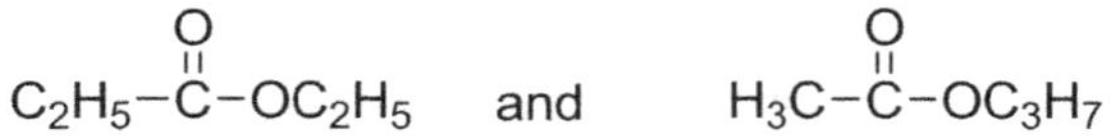

c) $C_2H_5-\overset{O}{\overset{||}{C}}-OC_2H_5$ and $H_3C-\overset{O}{\overset{||}{C}}-OC_3H_7$

5. Ring Chain Isomerism: In which one is with open chain structures and another is ring chain structure.

a) 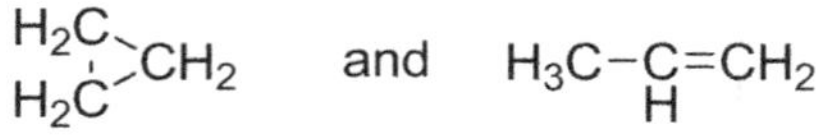 $\underset{H_2C}{\overset{H_2C}{>}}CH_2$ and $H_3C-\underset{H}{\overset{}{C}}=CH_2$

b) 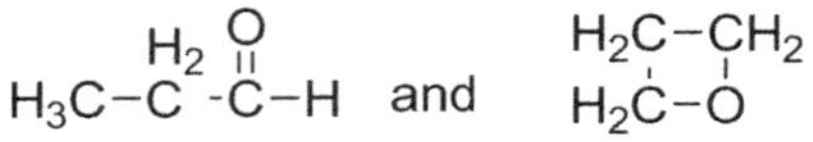 $H_3C-\overset{H_2}{C}-\overset{O}{\overset{||}{C}}-H$ and $\begin{matrix} H_2C-CH_2 \\ | \quad | \\ H_2C-O \end{matrix}$

Ib. Stereo-isomers: Same structure and same molecular formula, but differ in spatial arrangement of atoms or groups are called stereo-isomers. e.g.: 1,2-dichloroethylene

$$\underset{H\ \ H}{\overset{Cl\ \ Cl}{C=C}} \longleftrightarrow \underset{H\ \ Cl}{\overset{Cl\ \ H}{C=C}}$$

1. Enantiomers: The stereo isomers which are non-super imposable mirror images.

$$\underset{CH_3}{\overset{COOH}{H{-}{+}{-}OH}} \quad\Big|\quad \underset{CH_3}{\overset{COOH}{HO{-}{+}{-}H}}$$

non-superimposable mirror images

2. Diastereomers: Which are not mirror images.

not mirror images

Geometrical Isomers: Nomenclature of the geometrical isomers

$$\underset{1\ \ \ 2}{C=C} \quad \underset{1\ \ \ 2}{C=N{-}} \quad \underset{1\ \ 2}{{-}N=N{-}}$$

Substitution on C(1) C(2)		Geometrical isomerism	Nomenclature
aa	aa	No isomerism	---
aa	bb	No isomerism	---
aa	bc	No isomerism	---
aa	bb	$\underset{b\ \ \ \ b}{\overset{a\ \ \ \ a}{C=C}}$ cis $\underset{b\ \ \ \ a}{\overset{a\ \ \ \ b}{C=C}}$ trans	cis – trans

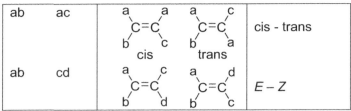

Nomenclature of Geometric isomers: [E – Z] nomenclature:

$$\begin{array}{c} a \\ \diagdown \\ b \end{array} C=C \begin{array}{c} c \\ \diagup \\ d \end{array} \qquad \begin{array}{c} a \\ \diagdown \\ b \end{array} C=C \begin{array}{c} d \\ \diagup \\ c \end{array}$$

To assign 'E' or 'Z' nomenclature we have to follow priority rule of Cahn-Ingold-Prelog sequence rule.

Cahn-Ingold-Prelog sequence rules:
(1) Priorities are given based on atomic number of directly attached atoms, whereas atomic number is more priority is more i.e. first priority. Accordingly 1st priority is > 2nd priority.
e.g.:

$$=C \begin{array}{c} Cl \ (1) \\ \diagup \\ \diagdown \\ H \ (2) \end{array} \qquad =C \begin{array}{c} CH_3 \ (2) = C \\ \diagup \\ \diagdown \\ OCH_3 \ (1) = O \end{array}$$

(2) If atomic numbers are same priorities are given based on atomic weights.

$$=C \begin{array}{c} H \ (2) \\ \diagup \\ \diagdown \\ D \ (1) \end{array}$$

D = deuterium

(3) If atomic numbers and atomic weights are same then priorities are given based on next atom or second atom.

$$=C \begin{array}{c} (2) \\ CH_3 \ (2) = C \\ \diagup \\ \diagdown \\ CCl_3 \ (1) = Cl \\ (1) \end{array} \qquad =C \begin{array}{c} (1) \\ CH_2OH \ (1) = O \\ \diagup \\ \diagdown \\ CD_3 \qquad (2) = C \\ (2) \end{array}$$

(4) Priority given for triple bond than double bond than single bond when bonded atom is same with different bonds.

$$\begin{array}{c} (1) \\ HC=O \\ =C \\ H_2C-OH \\ (2) \end{array} \quad \begin{array}{l} (1) = O \text{ (double bond)} \\ (2) = O \text{ (single bond)} \end{array} \quad \begin{array}{c} (2) \\ H_2C-NH_2 \\ =C \\ C\equiv N \\ (1) \end{array}$$

$$\begin{array}{c} H_3C \quad CH_3 \\ (2)C-CH_3 \\ =C \\ (1)C\equiv CH \end{array} \quad \begin{array}{c} H \quad CH_3 \\ (2)C-CH_3 \\ =C \\ HC=CH_2 \\ (1) \end{array}$$

(5) After assigning the priority numbers then the nomenclature will be assigned: If a (1) and c (1) are same side then it is Z – isomer (Z, from German *Zusammen* = together or same side). If a (1) and c (1) are opposite side then it is E – isomer (E, from German *Entgegen* = opposite).

$$\begin{array}{cc} (1)\,a & c\,(1) \\ & C=C \\ (2)\,b & d\,(2) \\ & \text{Z- isomer} \end{array} \qquad \begin{array}{cc} (1)\,a & d\,(2) \\ & C=C \\ (2)\,b & c\,(1) \\ & \text{E- isomer} \end{array}$$

Example of E – Z isomerism.

$$\begin{array}{cc} (2) & (2) \\ H & H_2C-NH_2 \\ & C=C \\ D & C\equiv CH \\ (1) & (1) \\ & \text{Z - isomer} \end{array} \qquad \begin{array}{cc} (1) & O\;(2) \\ H_2N & \overset{\parallel}{CH} \\ & \triangle \\ N\equiv C & F \\ (2) & (1) \\ & \text{E - isomer} \end{array}$$

$$\begin{array}{cc} (1) & (1) \\ Ph & OH \\ & C=N: \\ H & \\ (2) & (2) \\ & \text{Z - isomer} \end{array} \longleftrightarrow \begin{array}{cc} (1) & (2) \\ Ph & : \\ & C=N \\ H & H \\ (2) & (1) \\ & \text{E - isomer} \end{array} \quad \begin{array}{l} \text{always lone-pair} \\ \text{is given } 2^{nd} \\ \text{priority} \end{array}$$

(1) Ph (2)
   N=N
(2)   Ph (1)
   E - isomer

(1) H₃C   O (1)
         C=C   CH
(2) H   CH₃ (2)
  (trans) - Z - isomer

(1) O   (2)

(2) (1)
        Br
E - isomer

Cl (1)   (1) O

  (2)   (2)
   Z - isomer

(1)   (2)
ClH₂C   H   (2)
      (1) CH₃
H₃C (1)
 (2) H   CH₂CH₃
      (2) (1)
E - isomer; Z - isomer

H

H
cis - isomer

  Br

    Br
cis - isomer

   ,,Br

    ''Br
cis - isomer

   Br

    ''Br
trans - isomer

5.2. Dynamic Isomers

The isomers readily inter-convertible at room temperature.

IIa. Dynamic Structural isomers: Dynamic functional isomers

e.g.: keto-enol tautomers of Ethyl acetoacetate

$$H_3C-\overset{O}{\underset{}{C}}-\overset{H_2}{\underset{}{C}}-CO_2Et \underset{tautomers}{\overset{keto-enol}{\rightleftharpoons}} H_3C-\overset{OH}{\underset{}{C}}=\overset{}{\underset{H}{C}}-CO_2Et$$

keto-form   enol-form

IIb. Dynamic Stereo isomers: The stereo isomers which are inter-convertible at room temperature. For example conformational isomers – the isomers which are obtained by C – C single bond rotation.

e.g.: Alkanes and their compounds. Eclipsed and staggered are known as dynamic stereo isomers and these are **not mirror images** to each other so these are **Diastereo isomers**.

Fischer - projection   Newman - projections

C_2H_6 (Ethane)

eclipsed (0°) — less stable (more energetic)

staggered (60°) — more stable (less energetic)

C_4H_{10} (n-Butane)

eclipsed (0°) (I) — staggered (60°) Gauche (II) — partially eclipsed (120°) (III) — staggered (180°) Anti (IV)

Always staggered forms are more stable than eclipsed. Order of stability is IV > II > III > I. Energy differences are IV to II is 0.9 kcal; IV to III is 3.5 kcal; IV to I is 4.4 to 6.1 kcal. All these are Diastereo isomers.

Gauche (60°)　　　　　Gauche (300° or 60°)
mirror images (non-superimposable)

Gauche (60°) and Gauche (300° or 60°) of Newman projection isomers are non-super imposable **mirror images** so these are

Enantiomers and more specifically these are **Dynamic Enantiomers**.

6. Stereochemistry Advanced

1Q. What is stereoisomerism?

A. Stereoisomers are compounds made up of the same atoms bonded by the same sequence of bonds but having different three-dimensional structures which are not interchangeable.

These three-dimensional structures are called configurations.

2Q. What is the relationship between symmetry and chirality?

A. Asymmetric objects are chiral. Symmetric objects are achiral.

3Q. What is the relationship between objects and their mirror images?

A. symmetric objects are superposable with their mirror images. They are one and the same. Asymmetric objects are nonsuperposable with their mirror images. They are different objects.

In the case of molecules, chiral molecules and their mirror images are different molecules. Chiral molecules and their mirror images are a kind of stereoisomers called enantiomers.

4Q. What is optical activity?

A. Any material that rotates the plane of polarized light (polarimeter) is said to be optically active. If a pure compound is optically active, the molecule is nonsuperimposable on its mirror image. All chiral molecules are optically active.

If a molecule superimposable on its mirror image, the compound does not rotate the plane of polarized light; it is optically inactive. All achiral molecules, meso-compounds, racemic mixtures are optically inactive.

5Q. What is dextrorotatory and levorotatory?

A. Ability of chiral substances to rotate the plane of polarized light to the right is called **dextrorotatory**.
It is denoted with a sign of (+) or 'd' (small d) but, not capital D.
Ability of chiral substances to rotate the plane of polarized light to the left is called **levorotatory**. It is denoted with a sign of (-) or 'l' (small l) but, not capital L.

6Q. What is optical rotation and specific optical rotation? What factors will affect the rotation.

A. Optical activity is a specific property, so it is measured in specific rotation.
The factors effecting on optical rotation are: solvent, temperature, wavelength of light used, concentration of solution, length of tube (decimeter) (100 mm).

$$[\alpha]^t_D = \alpha / l \times c$$

Where; $[\alpha]$ = specific optical rotation, t = temperature (room temperature), D = wavelength of light (589nm)

α = optical rotation, l = length of the tube (decimeter) 100 mm, c = concentration of the solution.

Temperature: it should be always room temperature

Wave length of the light: is is constant for sodium vapor lamp with 589 nanometers

Solvent: solvent will be water for water soluble compounds and usually EtOH or MeOH or other organic solvent like $CHCl_3$, Et_2O etc., for other organic solvent soluble compounds.

So, even by changing concentration or length of the tube the optical rotation will change but specific optical rotation remains constant.

e.g., if a compound shows optical rotation 'α' of 20°, concentration (c = 1), tube length (l = 1 decimeter), wave length of light (D = 589 constant), temperature (t = 25°C, room temperature constant), then the specific optical rotation ([α]) is:

$[α]^{25}_{589} = 20 / 1×1 = 20°$

If concentration is changed to 2 (c = 2) then $[α]_D^{25} = 40 / 1×2 = 20°$.

7Q. How will you write the specific optical rotation observed for molecule?

A.

D-(+)- Glyceraldehyde   (R)-2,3-dihydroxypropanal

Specific optical rotation of D-(+)-Glyceraldehyde: $[α]_D^{25}$ +8.7° (c 2 in H_2O).

Where: D = Fischer projection notation; (+) = sign of rotation, 'd' or dextro-rotation; $_D$ = wave length of light used (589 nm) constant; 25 = room temperature (constant); +8.7° = value of optical rotation(+ = dextro); c 2 = concentration 2 (200 mg in 10 mL of solvent); H_2O = solvent (here water).

```
    CHO              CHO              OH
    (S)              (S)                              OHC  (S)  CH₂OH
HO—├—H          HO—═—H         OHC  (S)  CH₂OH            ═
    CH₂OH            CH₂OH                                OH

L-(-)-Glyceraldehyde             (S)-2,3-dihydroxypropanal
```

Specific optical rotation of L-(-)-Glyceraldehyde: $[\alpha]_D^{25}$ -8.7° (c 2 in H_2O).

Where: L = Fischer projection notation; (-) = sign of rotation, 'd' or dextro-rotation; $_D$ = wave length of light used (589 nm) constant; 25 = room temperature (constant); -8.7° = value of optical rotation(- = leavo); c 2 = concentration 2 (200 mg in 10 mL of solvent); H_2O = solvent (here water).

```
    CO₂H             CO₂H             OH                 OH
    (S)              (S)                                 
HO—├—H          HO—═—H         HO₂C  (S)  CO₂H     HO₂C (S) (S) CO₂H
H—├—OH          H—═—OH               OH                  OH
    CO₂H             CO₂H

D-(-)-Tartaric acid             (2S,3S)-2,3-dihydroxysuccinic acid
```

Specific optical rotation of D-(-)-Tartaric acid: $[\alpha]_D^{20}$ -12.0° (c 20 in H_2O).

Where: D = Fischer projection notation; (-) = sign of rotation, '*l*' or leavo-rotation; $_D$ = wave length of light used (589 nm) constant; 20 = room temperature (constant); -12.0° = value of optical rotation (- = leavo); c 20 = concentration 20 (2000 mg or 2 g in 10 mL of solvent); H_2O = solvent (here water).

$$\text{L-(+)-Tartaric acid} \longleftrightarrow \longleftrightarrow \longleftrightarrow \text{(2R,3R)-2,3-dihydroxysuccinic acid}$$

Specific optical rotation of L-(+)-Tartaric acid: $[\alpha]_D^{20}$+12.4° (c 20 in H_2O).

Where: L = Fischer projection notation; (+) = sign of rotation, 'd' or dextro-rotation; $_D$ = wave length of light used (589 nm) constant; 20 = room temperature (constant); +12.4° = value of optical rotation (+ = dextro); c 20 = concentration 20 (2000 mg or 2 g in 10 mL of solvent); H_2O = solvent (here water).

8Q. What is *asymmetric carbon atom*?

A. The traditional name (van't Hoff) for a carbon atom that is attached to four different entities (atoms or groups) e.g. C*abcd*.

9Q. What is *chirality*?

A. The property of nonsuperimposability of an object on its mirror image is called chirality.

Such molecule has no symmetry elements of the second kind (a mirror plane, σ = S_1, a centre of inversion, i = S_2, a rotation-reflection axis, S_{2n}). If the molecule is superposable on its mirror image, it is achiral.

10Q. What are the criteria for optical activity?

A. (1) To exhibit optical activity molecule must possess asymmetric carbon: Asymmetric carbon compounds are optically active. But, presence of asymmetric is not only the requirement.

Asymmetry:
if asymmetric centre present = optically active (may / may not check for other criteria)
if asymmetric centre absent = optically inactive (may / may not check for other criteria)

H–C(H)(H)–H	H–C*(COOH)(CH₃)–OH	H–C*(CH₃)–OH / H–C*(CH₃)–OH	H₃C–C(H)=C=C(H)–CH₃
absent inactive	present active	present but inactive plane of symmetry	no asymmetric carbon but optically active due to allene bond

(2) To exhibit optical activity molecule must not have the symmetry elements:

(a) plane of symmetry

(b) centre of symmetry

(c) n-fold alternating access of symmetry.

If these three are absent then only the compounds exhibits optical activity.

(a) Plane of symmetry: a plane which bisects the molecules into two mirror images are called plane of symmetry. If the plane of symmetry is present then the molecule is optically inactive, if absent then optically active.

Plane of symmetry:
if present = optically inactive; if absent = optically active

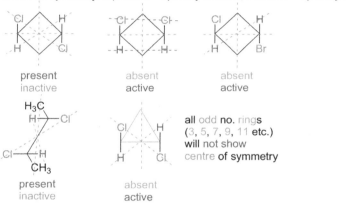

(b) Centre of symmetry: If all the lines two identical groups pass through a single point or a central point is called centre of symmetry.

Centre of symmetry: if present = optically inactive; if absent = optically active

(c) n-Fold alternating access of symmetry: If a rotation by 360°/n degrees (n = 1, 2, 3, …)followed by reflection in plane perpendicular to the access taken results in identical molecule the compound said to be possess n-fold alternating access of symmetry.

If plane of symmetry or centre of symmetry is present then n-fold alternative access of symmetry is present.

If plane of symmetry or centre of symmetry are absent then n-fold alternating access of symmetry will be absent.

If the n-fold alternating access of symmetry present then the molecule is optically inactive, if absent then optically active.

Allenes are optically active because absence of plane of symmetry. However, if on first or third carbon two same groups present it will be inactive.

$$\underset{\underset{H}{H_3C}}{}C=C=\underset{\underset{CH_3}{H}}{}$$
active

$$\underset{\underset{H_3C}{H_3C}}{}C=C=\underset{\underset{CH_3}{H}}{}$$
inactive
(1st carbon same 2 Me)

$$\underset{\underset{H}{C_2H_5}}{}C=C=\underset{\underset{C_2H_5}{H}}{}$$
active

$$\underset{\underset{H_3C}{H_3C}}{}C=C=\underset{\underset{C_2H_5}{H}}{}$$
inactive
(1st carbon same 2 Me)

$$\underset{\underset{C_2H_5}{H_3C}}{}C=C=\underset{\underset{C_2H_5}{C_2H_5}}{}$$
inactive
(3rd carbon same 2 Et)

11Q. How many optical isomers are possible for one chiral carbon containing compounds?

A. If n = number of chiral centers, the maximum possible number of stereoisomers is 2^n.

n	1	2	3	4	5
2^n	2	4	8	16	32

$$\begin{array}{c} CHO \\ H-\overset{*}{C}-OH \\ CH_2OH \end{array}$$
D-(+)-glyceraldehyde

$$\begin{array}{c} CHO \\ HO-\overset{*}{C}-H \\ CH_2OH \end{array}$$
L-(-)-glyceraldehyde

For example, CHO-CH(OH)-CH$_2$OH (glyceraldehydes) for this molecule n = 1 then 2^1 = 2. Therefore for glyceraldehydes two optical isomers are possible. D-(+)-glyceraldehyde and L-(-)-glyceraldehyde are non-super-imposable mirror images and these two are called *enantiomers*.

12Q. What are the differences between enantiomers?

A. Non superimposable mirror image isomers called enantiomers. For example D-(+)-glyceraldehyde and L-(-)-glyceraldehyde

$$\begin{array}{c} \text{CHO} \\ \text{H}-\overset{|}{\text{C}}-\text{OH} \\ \text{CH}_2\text{OH} \end{array} \qquad \begin{array}{c} \text{CHO} \\ \text{HO}-\overset{|}{\text{C}}-\text{H} \\ \text{CH}_2\text{OH} \end{array}$$

D-(+)-glyceraldehyde   L-(-)-glyceraldehyde

Physical and chemical property	D-(+)-glyceraldehyde	L-(-)-glyceraldehyde
Sign of optical rotation	Different, here dextro rotatory or	Different, here dextro rotatory or (-

	(+) or 'd'. $[\alpha]_D^{25}$ +8.7° (c 2 in H_2O).	) or 'l'. $[\alpha]_D^{25}$ -8.7° (c 2 in H_2O).
Thin layer chromatography	not separable, same Rf	not separable, same Rf
1H NMR, 13C NMR	No difference	No difference
LCMS, HPLC, GCMS	Same, no difference	Same, no difference
Melting point, boiling point, solubility, refractive index	Same, no difference	Same, no difference
Rate of reaction in achiral medium	Same rate of reaction	Same rate of reaction
Rate of reaction in chiral medium	Different in chiral medium	Different in chiral medium

13Q. What is meso form/meso compound?

A. Molecules that contain two or more chiral centers and at least one plane of symmetry are called meso forms these compounds are optically inactive. Cis-disubstituted cyclohexanes are examples of meso forms. Since these molecules have symmetry, they cannot have enantiomers. They are one and the same with their mirror images.

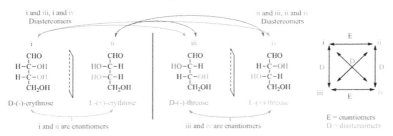

Cis-1,2-dichlorocyclohexane superposable mirror images (optically inactive)

meso compound (inactive)

meso tartaric acid (inactive)

meso compound (inactive)

meso-2,3-dibromobutane superposable mirror images (optically inactive)

14Q. What are diastereomer / diastereomers / diastereoisomerism?

A. Stereoisomerism other than enantiomerism. Diastereoisomers (or diastereomers) are stereoisomers not related as mirror images. Diastereoisomers are characterized by differences in physical properties, and by some differences in chemical behavior towards achiral as well as chiral reagents.

If two molecules are mirror images, then their configurations are exactly opposite and they are enantiomers. For example D and L erythroses are mirror images, so they are enantiomers, same way D and L threoses are enantiomers.

If two molecules are not mirror images, but still they are stereoisomers they are diastereomers, D-erythrose and D-threose are not mirror images so they are diastereomers, same way D-erythrose and L-threoses; L-erythrose and D-threose; L-erythrose and L-threoses are diastereomeric pairs.

Any molecule will have only one enantiomeric pair. But 2^n numbers of diastereomeric pairs are possible.

Physical and chemical property	Diastereomeric pair
Sign of optical rotation	Different
Thin layer chromatography	separable, different Rf
1H NMR, 13C NMR	Different δ values
LCMS, HPLC, GCMS	different
Melting point, boiling point, solubility, refractive index	different
Rate of reaction in achiral medium	different
Rate of reaction in chiral medium	different

Diastereomers are different geometrical entities. But enantiomers are identical geometrical entities.

For the diastereomeric relationship chirality is not essentiality.

For the diastereomeric relationship chirality is not essentiality. For example cis- and trans-isomers are diastereomers.

$$\underset{\text{cis}}{\overset{ClCl}{\underset{HH}{\diagup=\diagdown}}} \qquad \underset{\text{trans}}{\overset{HCl}{\underset{ClH}{\diagup=\diagdown}}}$$

'D' and 'L' are always enantiomers. 'd' and 'l' pair is enantiomeric pair.

Meso and active are diastereomers.

Single asymmetric centre cannot show diastereoisomerism.

Erythro and threo-isomers are always diastereomers.

Epimers are also diastereomers.

15Q. what are epimers.

A. Diastereomers that have the opposite configuration at only one of two or more tetrahedral stereogenic centres present in the respective molecular entities. For example D-glucose and D-mannose are epimers.

```
       CHO                    CHO
   ┌─────────┐            ┌─────────┐
   │ H-C-OH  │            │ HO-C-H  │
   └─────────┘            └─────────┘
    HO-C-OH                HO-C-H
    H──OH                  H──OH
    H──OH                  H──OH
    CH₂OH                  CH₂OH
   D-glucose              D-mannose
```

16Q. What is conformation?

A. The spatial arrangement of the atoms affording distinction between stereoisomers which can be interconverted by rotations about formally single bonds.

Any new shapes or geometries obtained by C-C bond rotations in space called as conformations. These are written in Newmann projection.

Newmann projection of D-tartaric acid eclipsed, gauche and staggered conformations

Fischer projection — D-tartaric acid — eclipsed — clock wise 60° rotation of back side carbon — gauche — clock wise two 60° rotation of back side carbon — staggered

17Q. What is configuration and what is absolute configuration and relative configuration

A. In the context of stereochemistry, the term is restricted to the arrangements of atoms of a molecular entity in space that distinguishes stereoisomers, the isomerism between which is not due to conformation difference.

Determination of special arrangement of groups at asymmetric centre is called configuration.

Configuration will be described by 'R' or 'S', in Fischer projection 'D' and 'L', for alkenes 'E' and 'Z'

Absolute configuration:

The spatial arrangement of the atoms of a chiral a molecular entity (or group) and its stereochemical description e.g. R or S.

Without taking any reference molecule if configuration of given molecule determined by means of X-ray crystallography.

Alternatively it can be determined by 'Optical rotatory dispersion', 'vibrational circular dichroism' and by the use of chiral shift reagents in proton NMR. When the absolute configuration is obtained the assignment of R or S is based on the Cahn-Igngol-Prelog priority rules.

If the name of a compound includes both the sign of rotation and the designation 'R' or 'S' then the absolute configuration of that compound is known.

Relative Configuration:

By using some reference compounds (e.g. amino acids or carbohydrates) if configuration of given molecule is determined the configuration is called relative configuration.

The arrangement of atoms in an optically active molecule, based on chemical inter-conversion from or to a known compound, is relative configuration.

Et		Et		Et	CHO		CHO
HO–C(H)(CH₃)	TsCl, pyridine →	TsO–C(H)(CH₃)	KCN, ethanol →	H–C(CN)(CH₃)	H—OH CH₂OH	⇒	H—C—OH HO—C—OH H—OH CH₂OH
(R)-(−)		(R)		(S)	D-glyceraldehyde		D-glucose

The reaction of an alcohol with TsCl is known to occur with retention of configuration that is the group priority of the stereogenic center has not been altered. The reaction of the tosylate with nitrile occurs with inversion, as a result the group priority at the stereogenic center has been altered.

The absolute configuration of the parent is known while only the relative configurations of the tosylate and the nitrile are known.

18Q. What are the ways to write molecular representations?

A. Organic molecules are three dimensional (3D) this 3D cannot be shown on 2D plane of a paper or board.

In general plain lines —— depict bonds approximately in the plane of the drawing; bonds to atoms above the plane are shown with a bold wedge ◄— or a bold bond ▬ may be use; and bonds to atoms below the plane are shown with short parallel line ⁞⁞⁞⁞⁞ but not --- (it is used for partial bond or hydrogen bonding). If stereochemistry unknown this can be indicated by a wavy line ∿. Other specific methods include Fischer projection, Newman projection, sawhorse projection and wedge projection.

19Q. What is Fischer projection and how will you write these representations?

A. In Fischer projection each asymmetric carbon in the molecule must be represented in the form of cross †. Every Fischer projection will have one vertical line and one or more than one horizontal lines. Arrange maximum number of carbons on vertical line. Keep *more oxidized carbon at the top of vertical line*. The groups on vertical line are below the plane. The groups on horizontal line are above the plane. All C-C bonds at the crosses are in plane.

Fischer projection	Wedge projection	Fischer projection	Wedge projection
CHO H–C–OH H–C–OH CH$_2$OH	CHO H►C◄OH H►C◄OH CH$_2$OH	CHO HO–C–H H–C–OH CH$_2$OH	CHO HO►C◄H H►C◄OH CH$_2$OH
D-erythrose	D-erythrose	D-threose	D-threose

The carbon with more number of oxygen or less number of hydrogen is the highly oxidized carbon. Any Fischer projection is eclipsed Fischer projection ($\theta = 0°$).

Rotation of Fischer projection (in plane) by 180° will not change configurations. Rotation of Fischer projection (in plane) by 90° converts into its *enantiomer*. Exchange of any two groups at the asymmetric centre on Fischer projection changes the configuration but exchange of any three groups at asymmetric centre in will not change configuration.

CO$_2$H H$_3$N─┼─H CH$_3$ I	3 exchanges ----►	CO$_2$H H─┼─CH$_3$ NH$_2$ II	CO$_2$H H$_3$N─┼─H CH$_3$ I	2 exchanges ----►	CO$_2$H H─┼─NH$_2$ CH$_3$ III
I and II are identical			I and III are not identical

While writing mirror image of Fischer projection oppose the groups at horizontal lines, vertical groups unaffected.

20Q. What is Fischer's 'D' and 'L' configuration and how will you differentiate them?

A. In the Fischer projection 'D' and 'L" are arbitrary chosen letters (do not confuse with 'd' and 'l' which are sign of optical rotation). D and L configuration is valid for only Fischer projection and these can be depicted by seeing the structure.

Rules for Fischer projection: If more electronegative group at bottommost asymmetric centre on the right side the configuration is 'D'. If it is on the left side then it's configuration is 'L'.

Fischer projection

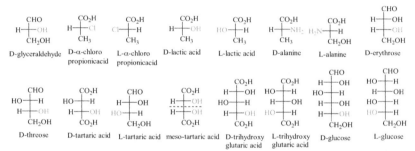

D and L compounds are enantiomers.

21Q. What is C. I. P. system or CIP priority and what are their rules?

A. It is a short form for Cahn-Ingold-Prelog (CIP) priority rules system. CIP system or CIP conventions are a set of rules used to name the stereoisomers of a molecule. A molecule may contain any number of stereocenters and any number of double bonds and each gives rise to two possible configurations. The purpose of the CIP system is to assign 'R' (Rectus means clock wise) and 'S' (Sinister means anti-clock wise) descriptor to each sterocenter and an 'E' or 'Z' descriptor to each double bond so that the configuration of the entire molecule can be specified uniquely by including the descriptors in its systematic name.

The CIP sequence rules are: (1) Give priority (numbering) to the groups at the asymmetric centre based on atomic weight of an atom which is directly attached to asymmetric centre, i.e. more atomic weight atom given first priority.

(2) If atomic weights of directly attached atoms are same, then chose other atoms in the group in sequence, e.g. CH_2CH_3 is more priority then CH_3.

(3) If multiple bonded groups attached to asymmetric centre do the duplication and triplication of the group.

(4) If asymmetric centre attached 'R' and 'S' configuration groups, then the carbon having 'R' configuration should be given priority over 'S'.

(5) if there is a 'E' and 'Z' configuration groups at asymmetric centre then the carbon with 'Z' should be given more priority over 'E'.

22Q. What is 'R' and 'S' configuration?

A. R and S notations are used only to describe asymmetric molecules following CIP sequence rules.

Step I: first we assign the priority numbers to the four atoms/groups attached to chiral centre according to CIP rules. For example in the case of CHClBrI, the four atoms attached to the chiral center are all different and priority will be given based on atomic weight, thus the priority follows as I, Br, Cl, H.

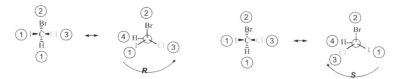

Step 2: In Fischer projection representation orient the molecule so that the least priority group must be on lower end of vertical line. If the lower priority group on horizontal line or upper side on vertical line, then to bring the group on to vertical line do two

mutual exchanges of groups so that the least priority group come to lower end of vertical line.

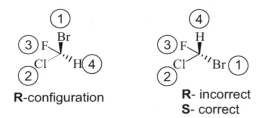

| D-glyceraldehyde | D-glyceraldehyde R-configuration | L-glyceraldehyde | D-glyceraldehyde S-configuration |

Step 3: After giving priority order for the groups at asymmetric centre, if priority direction is clockwise the configuration is specified '**R**' (Latin: *rectus*, right); if anticlockwise the configuration is specified '**S**' (Latin: *sinister*, left).

Step 4: On wedge projection if least priority group is below the plane or represented as ||||| away from the observer then assign the configuration according to priority rules without changing the orientation.

R-configuration

R- incorrect
S- correct

If on wedge projection least priority group is above the plane or represented as — or ◄ or rear side to the observer, then oppose the configuration.

23Q. How will you assign the R and S notations to the molecules without changing the orientation?

A. After assigning the priority numbers at asymmetric carbon, If the priority numbers shows anticlockwise but the least priority group is not at down or below the plane then the configuration will be 'R' and it can be proved by two mutual exchanges of groups so that the least priority group orient down on vertical line.

If the priority numbers shows clockwise but the least priority group is not at down or below the plane then the configuration will be S and it can be proved by two mutual exchanges of groups so that the least priority group orient down on vertical line. So now the L-thryose is denoted as *(2R,3S)-2,3,4-trihydroxybutanal.*

24Q. What is *cis-trans* isomerism?

A. *Cis-trans* isomerism [geometrical isomerism (this term not in use), configurational isomerism] is used to designate the absolute configuration around double bond (olefins) or cycloalkanes (or hetero-analogues) following the CIP priority rules.

| cis | trans | no cis-trans isomerism | | trans | cis-azoxy benzene |

If the priority atoms/group is on the same side then it is denoted as *cis-* (Latin: on this side; same side). If the priority atoms/group is on the opposite side then it is denoted as *trans-* (Latin: on other side; opposite side).

Question Answers:
Chapter 1: Structure of Organic Molecules
1. Q. What is the Ground state valency of Carbon?
Ans. Carbon Ground State Valency is 2.
2. Q. What is the hybridization of CO carbon monoxide and CO_2 carbon dioxide?
Ans. Carbon monoxide CO hybridization is SP, Carbon dioxide CO_2 hybridization is SP.
3. Q. What is the hybridization of Carbocation and Carbanion?
Ans. Carbocation Hybridization is SP2. Carbanion Hybridization is SP3.
4. Q. How many lone pairs of electrons are there in water molecule and how to calculate them?
Ans. Lone pair of electrons of a molecule can be calculated by the general formula as:
Group number of an atom in periodic table – total number of bonds around that atom
= no. of electrons which upon divided by 2 gives
= no. of lone pair electrons.
water H_2O = Oxygen = 6 – 2 = 4 divided by 2 = 2

That means no. of lone pair electrons in water molecules is 2.

5. Q. What is the Hybridization of NH_3 ammonia and ammonium chloride NH_4Cl?

Ans. Hybridization of NH_3 ammonia is SP3. Hybridization of ammonium chloride NH_4Cl is SP3

6. Q. What is the CC Bond Length of SP3, SP2 and SP Hybridization?

Ans. C-C single bond length = 1.54 Angstroms
C=C double bond length = 1.34 Angstroms
C≡C triple bond length = 1.21 Angstroms

7. Question: How the bond length changes in a group going from top to bottom?

Ans. In a group as electro negativity decreases so the bond length increases.

8. Q. What is the bond length of methyl chloride, methyl bromide and methyl iodide?

Ans. Methyl Chloride C-Cl bond length = 1.79 Angstroms Methyl Bromide C-Br bond length = 1.97 Angstroms Methyl Iodide C-I bond length = 2.16 Angstroms

9. Q. What happens to bond length in a period moving from left to right?

Ans. In periodic table as moving from left to right electro negativity increases so bond length decreases.

10. What factors affect the bond length?

Ans. Bond length is affected by Resonance and Hyperconjugation.

11. Q. What is the shape of SP3, SP2 and SP Hybridized molecules?

Ans. SP3:

(a) Tetrahedral (4 sigma bonds) for example methane molecule (CH4).

(b) Pyramidal (3 sigma bonds + 1 lone pair) for example ammonia molecule (NH3).

(c) Angular or V shape (2 sigma bonds + 2 lone pairs) for example water molecule (H2O).

SP2:

(a) Trigonal planar (3 sigma bonds) for example sulfurtrioxide molecule (SO3).

(b) Angular or V shape (2 sigma bonds + 1 lone pair) for example sulfurdioxide molecule (SO2).

SP: Linear (2 sigma bonds) for example acetylene molecule.

12. Q. What is bond energy of SP3, SP2 and SP hybridized molecules?

Ans. Bond Energy is the energy required to make or break a bond in a organic molecule. C-C: single bond energy: 81 k cal/mole. C=C: double bond energy: 146 k cal/mole. C≡C triple bond energy: 192 k cal/mole.

13. Q. What is bond angle of SP3, SP2 and SP hybridization.

Ans. Bond angle of

sp3 (109.28),

sp2 (120),

sp (180).

14. Q. What are the common hybridization is observed in organic molecules?

Answer: SP3, SP2 and SP. 5. Question: How to know planar and non-planar of molecule?

Ans. SP and SP2 are planar,

SP2 and SP3 are non-linear.

SP: planar and linear

SP2: planar but non-linear

SP3: non-planar and non-linear.

Chapter 2: Reactivity of Organic Molecules

1. Q. How free radicals are formed and what type of reactions they undergo?

Ans. In a reaction if bond fission takes place homolytically then the reaction will follow radical mechanism and the type of reactions will be either
(i) free radical substitution reaction (if substitution takes place) or
(ii) free radical addition reaction (if addition takes place).
2. Q. How ions are formed in an organic reaction and what type mechanism they follow?
Ans. If bond fission takes place heterolytically then the ions of cations and anions are formed and the reaction follows ionic mechanism.
3. Q. How many types of Reagents are there in Organic Chemistry?
Ans. Reagents are of three types they are:
(1) Free radical (all free radicals)
(2) Electrophilic reagents (all cations are positive electrophiles and all Lewis acids and carbenes are neutral electrophiles).
(3) Nucleophilic reagents (all anions are negative nucleophiles and all Lewis bases and organometalic compounds are neutral nucleophile).
Free radicals reacts with free radicals only and ions reacts with ions
4. Q. How many types of reactions are there in Organic Chemistry?
Ans. There are mainly 5 types reactions are there in Organic Chemistry and they are:
a. Substitution reactions (free radical substitution reaction, electrophilic substitution reaction, nucleophilic substitution reaction).
b. Addition reactions (free radical addition reaction, electrophilic addition reaction, nucleophilic addition reactions).
c. Elimination reactions (alpha-elimination reaction, beta-elimination reaction).
d. Molecular rearrangements (intra-molecular, inter-molecular).

e. Pericyclic reactions (electrocyclic, cycloaddition, sigmatropic reactions).

5. Q. What is main difference between electrophiles and nucleophiles?
Ans. Electrophiles are electron loving species, while Nucleophiles are electron donating species.

6. Q. How many stages are there in a Free Radical Substitution Reaction Mechanism and what are they?
Ans. Free Radical Substitution Reaction Mechanism involves 3 stages of initiation, propagation and termination.

7. Q. How many stages are there in a SE2 – Bimolecular Electrophilic Substitution Reaction Aromatic mechanism and what are they?
Ans. SE2 – Bimolecular Electrophilic Substitution Reaction Aromatic mechanism involves 3 stages of formation of electrophile, formation of sigma complex and Removal of H+.

8. Q. What type of reactions does aromatic compounds undergo?
Ans. Aromatic compounds undergoes mainly Electrophilic Substitution bimolecular Reactions SE2.

9. Q. What type of reaction is Friedel Crafts alkylation and acylation?
Ans. Friedel-Crafts Alkylation and Acylation reactions are examples of SE2.

10. Q. What type of reactions are these: nitration, sulphonation of aromatic compounds?
Ans. Nitration, Halogenation and Sulphonation of aromatic compounds is example of SE2.

11. Q. What is and what happens in SN1 Reaction Mechanism and how to write arrow mark?
Ans. SN1 – Unimolecular Nucleophilic Substitution Reaction mechanism involves 2 stages and rate of the reaction depends on concentration of Reactant and gives Racemic mixture. In Nucleophilic Substitution reactions arrow mark must be shown from reagent nucelophile to reactant.

12. Q. What is and what happens in SN2 Reaction Mechanism?
Ans. SN2 – Bimolecular Nucleophilic Substitution Reaction mechanism involves only 1 stage and rate of the reaction depends on concentration of Reactant and Reagent and gives inversion of configuration.
13. Q. What is and what happens in SNi Reaction Mechanism?
Ans. SNi – Intra-molecular Nucleophilic Substitution Reaction results retention of configuration.
14. Q. What happens to stereo isomers R and S in SN1, SN2 and SNi type of reactions?
Ans.
1. in SN1 reaction Racemisation takes place and - R isomer - gives - R + S racemic mixture.
2. In SN2 reaction Walden Inversion takes place - R isomer - gives - S isomer -Walden inversion .
3. In SNi reaction retention of configuration takes place - R isomer - gives - R isomer retention of configuration.

15. Q. What type of Reactions Alkenes undergo?
Ans. Alkenes always undergoes Electrophilic Addition Reaction.
16. Q. What type of Reactions Carbonyl Compounds undergo?
Ans. Carbonyl compounds always undergo Nucleophilic Addition Reaction.
17. Q. What is Grignard Reaction?
Ans. Grignard reaction is an example of Nucleophilic Addition Reaction.
18. Q. How many atoms or groups are added in Addition Reaction?
Ans. In Addition reactions two groups/atoms are added.
19. Q. What happens to Alkyle halides in presence of alcoholic KOH (potassium hydroxide)?
Ans. Alkyl halides in presence of alcoholic KOH undergo Elimination reaction.

20. Q. What happens to Alkyle halides in presence of aqueous KOH (potassium hydroxide)?
Ans. Alkyl halides in presence of aqueous KOH undergo Nucleophilic Substitution reaction.
21. Q. How many atoms or groups are eliminated in Elimination Reaction?
Ans. In Elimination reactions two groups or atoms are eliminated.
22. Q. Molecular Rearrangement where it takes place?
Ans. Molecular Rearrangement takes place in between adjacent carbons only.
23. Q. Is it Pericyclic Reactions are ionic or free radical type of reactions?
Ans. Pericyclic reactions are neither free radical nor ionic reaction.
24. Q. Under what conditions Pericyclic reactions are performed?
Ans. Pericyclic reactions are conducted under photochemical or thermal condition.

Chapter 3: Electronic Displacements
1. Q. What is Inductive Effect?
Ans. Inductive Effect is a partial polarization of electrons towards more electro negative atom or group in a sigma bond.
2. Q. How stability of carbocations is affected by Inductive Effect?
Ans. Positive Inductive Effecting groups such as methyl groups increases the stability of carbocations so tertiary is more stable than secondary than primary carbocation.
3. Q. How Acidity of carboxylic acids is affected by Inductive Effect?
Ans. Negative Inductive Effecting groups such as chloro increases the acidity of carboxylic acids.
4. Q. How basicity of amines is affected by Inductive Effect?
Ans. Positive Inductive Effecting groups such as methyl increases the basicity of amines.
5. Q. What is the basicity order of ammonia, trimethyl amine, methyl amine, dimenthyl amine?

Ans. In aqueous solution the basicity order of amines is as follows: more basic is dimethyl amine than methyl amine than trimethyl amine than ammonia.

6. Q. What is Hyperconjugation and where it is observed?
Ans. The delocalization of α alpha carbon σ sigma bond electrons is known as hyperconjugation and it is observed alpha to unsaturated carbon or free radical or carbocation.

7. Q. What is keto-enol tautomerism?
Ans. Carbonyl carbons especially aldehydes and ketones exhibit this tautomerism where ketone resonance stabilized by enol because of Hyperconjugation and it is observed only in alpha carbon containing molecules.
For example acetaldehyde shows the keto-enol tautomersim but not benzaldehyde because benzaldehyde does not have alpha carbon hydrogens.

8. Q. If an unsaturated carbon molecule has 3 hydrogens on alpha carbon then how many ransonance structures are possible?
Ans. Three resonance structures are possible.

9. Q. What is Inductomeric Effect?
Ans. Increase in inductive effect in the presence of a reagent is known as Inductomeric effect. It is a temporary effect.

10. Q. What is Electromeric Effect?
Ans. Mesomeric effect which is operated only in the presence of a reagent is known as electromeric effect.

Chapter 4: Acidity and Basicity

1. Q. What is Arrhenius acid?
Ans. Arrhenius acid is a compound which ionises in water to give H+ ions, for example HCl (hydrochloric acid).

2. Q. What is Arrhenius base?
Ans. Arrhenius base is a compound which ionises in water to give OH- ions, for example NaOH (sodium hydroxide).

3. Q. What is Bronsted-Lowry acid?

Ans. Bronsted-Lowry acid is a compound which donates a proton.
4. Q. What is Bronsted-Lowry base?
Ans. Bronsted-Lowry base is a compound which accepts a proton.
5. Q. What is Lewis acid?
Ans. Lewis acid is a compound which accepts lone pair of electrons, for example AlCl3 (Aluminium chloride).
6. Q. What is Lewis base?
Ans.: Lewis base is a compound which donates lone pair of electrons, for example NH3 (ammonia).
7. Q. What is pKa?
Ans.: pKa = -log10Ka Where Ka = acid dissociation constant.
8. Q. What is the relationship of pKa with acidity strength of an acid.
Ans.: The lower the pKa value, stronger the acid. That means pKa is inversely proportional to acidity strength of an acid.
9.Q. What are the acidic organic compounds and what is their pKa?
Ans.: There are four types of organic compounds are acidic in nature.
Carboxylic acids (pKa 1 to 5)
Phenols (pKa 10)
Alcohols (pKa 15)
Alkynes (pKa 25).
10.Q. What is pKa of sulphuric acid, hydrochloric acid and water and which more acidic?
Ans.: Sulphuric acid (H2SO4) pKa: - 10
Hydrochloric acid (HCl) pKa: - 5
Water (H2O) pKa = 15
Based on pKa strength it is clear that sulphuric acid is strong acid than hydrochloric acid and water.
11.Q. What is the pKa of carboxylic acids?

Ans. Carboxylic acids are strong organic acids and their pKA values range from 0 to 5. For example Trifluoro Acetic acid pKA is 0.23 and benzoic acid pKA is 4.20.

12. Q. What are factors affecting the acidity strength of carboxylic acids?

Ans. There are two factors which affect the acidity strength of carboxylic acids. They are:
1. Effect of chelation
2. Substituent nature and position.

13. Q. What is ortho effect?

Ans. In general irrespective of nature of substituent, ortho-substituted benzoic acids are more acidic than meta and para. This is due to ortho-effect: explained by steric-crowdiness.

The Substituent at ortho (or) para position can show it's electronic effect more effectively than the meta position.

14. Q. Among ortho salicylic acid and para salicylic acid which is more acidic and why?

Ans. Ortho salicylic acid is more acidic than para salicyclic acid because of chelation.

15. Q. Among Trifluoro acetic acid and acetic acid which more acidic and why?

Ans. Trifluoro acetic acid is more acidic than acetic acid because of electron withdrawing effect of fluoro substituent.

16. Q. What is the pKa of formic acid.

Ans. Formic acid pKa: 3.7.

17Q. Among ortho Nitro benzoic acid and ortho methyl benzoic acid which is more acidic and why?

Ans. Ortho Nitro benzoic acid is more acidic than ortho methyl benzoic acid because of electron withdrawing nature of nitro group.

18. Q. How the order of carboxylic acids acidity changes with substituent moving from top to bottom in periodic table?

Ans. Carboxylic acids acidity strength decreases moving from top to bottom in periodic table.

For example:
Fluoro acetic acid pKA: 2.65 (more acidic)
Chloro acetic acid pKA: 2.85
Bromo acetic acid pKA: 2.90.
Iodo acetic acid pKA: 3.10 (less acidic).
19. Q. Among benzoic acid and acetic acid which is more acidic?
Ans. Benzoic acid (pKa: 4.20) is more acidic than acetic acid (pKa: 4.74).
20. Q. What is super acid?
Ans. Trifluro acetic acid is also known as organic super acid.

Made in the USA
Monee, IL
22 January 2021